JESUS THE MAS†ER COACH

How the 100 QUESTIONS OF JESUS enable ANYONE, ANYWHERE, ANYTIME, to have LIFE-CHANGING INTERACTIONS

"...Did not our hearts **burn** within us while he talked to us on the road..."
Luke 24:32

Dr. Joseph Umidi

Jesus the Master Coach

How the 100 QUESTIONS OF JESUS enable
ANYONE, ANYWHERE, ANYTIME,
to have LIFE-CHANGING INTERACTIONS

©2019 Lifeforming Institute

ISBN: 978-0-9914824-9-8
(Also available for Kindle)

Cover design: 100Covers (100covers.com)
Layout and Pre-press: Lighthouse24

All scripture references are from
the New King James Version
unless otherwise noted.

Dedication

To the Core Partner Team who dreamed with me in our original partnership to bring coaching values and competencies into the world. Thank you Doug Fike and Tony Stoltzfus.

To the Staff at Transformational Leadership Coaching (Lifeforming) over the 22 years who have zigged and zagged with me and with the market. You have the perseverance of Job!

To the 100+ Trainers and 10,000+ certified coaches who have embraced your own transformation process instead of taking the short cut to the many quickie coaching programs on the market. Thank you for the hundreds of stories you have made happen, including the ones in this book.

To the Regent University coaching students who, along with others, have formed training centers in 31 countries and 15 languages. You are the pioneers of a global movement of life-changers.

To the Ambassador Association of high-impact leaders who are stewarding your influence as creative and courageous kingdom advancers. Thank you for your labor of love on these original categories of the 100 Questions of Jesus. This includes the organizational and spiritual leadership of VP Paco Garcia, the coach values editorial work of Lyn Eichmann, PCC, and the contextual example of 12/100 verses from Tom Martin. Favor, wisdom, and anointing is your legacy.

To my life-partner and bride who has stewarded your evangelism call through the Arts and have amazed me with the gospel presentation of "The Play", now in multiple languages in video. What you wrote, produced, and directed is giving hope to the most unreached peoples today. Your work with me on these questions with the video clip illustrations has made this my most creative work produced in my calling. I love you Marie!

To our family and our spiritual sons and daughters who will live their lives to the fullest as they stand on our shoulders and do what we could never have on our own. I know that you are only one question away from a breakthrough; either to you or through you.

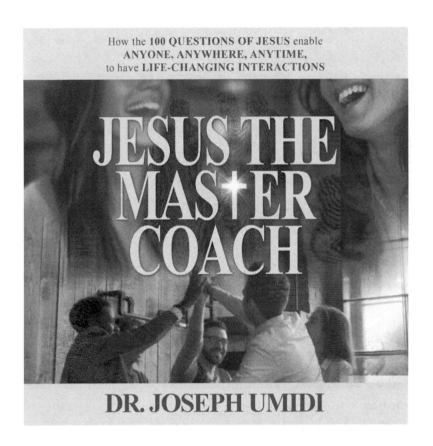

DOWNLOAD THE AUDIO BOOK FREE!

READ THIS FIRST

Just to say thanks for buying my book, I would like to give you the Audiobook version 100% FREE!

TO DOWNLOAD GO TO:

http://www.lifeforminginstitute.com/jmc/audiobook

Endorsements for
JESUS THE MASTER COACH

In his latest book, *Jesus the Master Coach: How the 100 Questions of Jesus enable anyone, anywhere, anytime, to have life-changing interactions,* Dr. Joseph Umidi distills his decades of teaching and coaching into a guide for anyone who wants to have a positive impact on the people around them. As Dr. Umidi writes, "the difference between a whole-hearted disciple and a half-hearted disciple can be found around the questions we are being asked and the questions we discover how to ask." Get this book and learn for yourself how to ask the right question at the right time and in the right way that will lead people to their own revelation.

—Gordon Robertson
CEO, the Christian Broadcasting Network

My good friend Joseph Umidi understands why discipling and coaching people into an intimate relationship with and likeness of Jesus is essential. He has built a life-long mission around this and has distilled the essential skills needed to do this in this book.

His insights are practical, profound, user friendly and loaded with wisdom. He has tapped into the essence of a transformational process using real life stories and technology that is engaging, creative and powerful.

Get this book, study it, apply it and pass it on to those in your world.

—Dr. Ron Jenson
America's Life Coach
Author, speaker, executive leadership coach
and Chairman of High Ground

This book, *Jesus the Master Coach* is written by another master coach my friend Joseph Umidi. The questions, not the answers in this book, will unlock the mysterious and bring focus to that which is fuzzy. Literally, a life time of wisdom is distilled for our benefit. You'll grow yourself and help others grow as well.

—Sam Chand,
Leadership Consultant and author of Leadership Pain

I have known Joseph Umidi for 20 years and he is without a doubt a man with great insights on leadership and coaching. He is a blessing to the body of Christ, solid in biblical knowledge, and is very practical in his insights. I would highly recommend his book to you!

—Pastor Steve Kelly,
Senior Pastor of Wave Church

I highly recommend to you my friend Joseph Umidi's new book, *Jesus The Master Coach*! This book is a treasure where we can glean from Joseph's lifetime of coaching experience. I look forward to using this book as a tool to guide me to ask the right questions to those I mentor and coach throughout the nations.

—Larry Kreider
DOVE International
International Director and author of over 40 books

The need for equipped Christian leaders, ministers and coaches to help answer the fundamental core questions of life and "what is God's Plan?" has never been greater.

In his book, Jesus the Master Coach, Dr. Umidi offers sound biblical answers to these age-old questions. From decades of ministry and mentoring comes his ability to lead and guide people straight to the source, Jesus. It gives me great pleasure to endorse this world changing book.

—Bishop Robert Stearns,
Executive Director, Eagles' Wings

The Master has birthed a Masterpiece through the meticulous and anointed work of Dr. Joseph Umidi. This groundbreaking work will provide Kingdom coaches across the globe access to open the hearts of men and women through the inerrant and infallible coaching questions of Jesus. Thank you Dr. Umidi for unleashing a revolution in the world of coaching.

—Christina Lee
National Speaker, Executive Leadership Coach & Certified Coach Trainer
President & Chief Operating Officer
Paradigm 360 Coach Training, LLC

My late husband Randy and I have known Joseph since the early years of our ministry as a friend and life coach. His very practical insight and powerful application of character development training has greatly influenced our Mission's leadership base. The role of a Christian leader in any area of life must be based on the biblical principles modeled by Jesus, which the author explains with great clarity for the one called to train, as well as the disciple to become the future trainer. Congrat-ulations Joseph, on a life-changing book that should be recommended material for all established and emerging churches.

—Marcy MacMillan
President, Federation of Churches Comunidad Cristiana de Fe,
Mission South America Convening Apostle,
Apostolic Commission Cali, Colombia

Dr. Umidi has skillfully crafted a profound procedure for his readers to systematically embrace positive changes in their conversation, countenance, and conduct. Read the book, apply the knowledge, and reap the benefits. This is a time-proven path to your success.

—Dr. Clarice Fluitt
Personal Advisor, Motivational Speaker, Author,
Television Personality, and Founder of Clarice Fluitt Ministries

The insights presented in this book are truly transformational. I have followed Dr. Joseph Umidi´s thoughtful and practical training for more than two decades, and I am forever grateful for its impact on both a personal and professional level. Truly recommended, guaranteed transformational!

—Øystein Gjerme
Senior Pastor, Salt Norway

Based on my education (a doctorate in theology and a master's in counseling) I believed that my function was to impart knowledge and wisdom to those who came to me for help as their pastor or leader. Dr. Umidi's Transformational Coaching course revealed the truth: My job was to coach them, which meant I needed to listen and ask questions more than I talked. (That was hard for me!) One of the most important components of this training was his brilliant revelations on the 100 questions that Jesus, the Master Coach, asked. If you want to be like Jesus and minister as He did, you will find this book to be indispensable.

—Dr. Tom Barrett
CEO Golden Art, LLC
Founder, Conservative Truth

Jesus' questions will come alive as you don the tri-focal glasses of biblical values, theology, and D.O.O.R. categories, and view afresh these well-known questions.

Simple, yet profound; easy to read, yet powerfully transformational; instructional, yet highly practical – *Jesus the Master Coach* is unlike any other book, building a roadway upon which you may walk together with the Holy Spirit, as He unveils to you yet another hidden aspect of the excellency of Christ, and transforms both you and your relationships, one conversation at a time!

—Dr. Les Brickman
Author, Kenya Missionary, Strategist

"Questions are the keys that unlock the mind to explore; open the eyes to comprehend and guide the heart to go beyond belief to trust. Prof Umidi is a Master Key-holder imitating the Lord Jesus Christ in enabling people to sift wisdom from knowledge and understanding to meaningful applications for life and eternity."

—Dr. Andrew Gho, Trainer, Consultant, Elder,
Board Member Haggai Institute, World Vision, Founder
Impact Magazine: Christian magazine with an Asian Perspective

"Questions are the basic unit of leadership transformation, and Dr. Umidi has sparked a global transformational movement. Exploring how great leaders impact others is one thing, framing conversational intelligence is another. This book will help you discover the underlying system through which Jesus impacted lives. Exploring the 100 questions with openness and diligence will lead you to the heart of leadership and closer to the heart of God!"

—Dr. Jesus A. Sampedro Hidalgo.
President - Global Leadership Consulting.
Leadership author, professor and LLC Coach-trainer.

This wonderful heart-level sharing is a culmination of decades of hard work, experience and dedication to our Lord. Living out his dream to mobilize Christian leaders and coaches to have a global impact, the author draws strongly from the greatest author of all, our Lord Jesus Christ, the true Master Coach.

—Swan Foo Boon
Chairman and Chief Executive Officer at
Singapore Consortium Investment Management Limited

I first met Dr. Umidi at a coach training session he taught in Singapore back in August 2019. By January, I was already passing on the truths that he imparted with great excitement to all 260 leaders in my church back in Malaysia with the compelling vision spreading the coaching movement here, and in the other 7 nations He has planted thus far. Jesus the Master Coach has been crafted with the busy pastor or leader in mind - it's easy to read and simple enough to understand - with many real stories and practical examples that come alongside biblically based principles and practices that are both powerful and prophetic. I truly believe what God has imparted to His servant, much of which is found in this book, will not only greatly benefit the churches that embrace it wholeheartedly and take them to a whole new level, just like it's doing for us, but that it will also revolutionize the way disciples are made and leaders are multiplied in our churches and organizations today - the way Jesus intended it to be in the first place.

—Rev. Kenneth Chin
Founding Senior Pastor, Acts Church, Kuala Lumpur
Founding Director, Asian Youth Ambassadors, Malaysia

Dr. Umidi produced a Double-Diamond gem. Jesus the Master Coach personifies the heartbeat and mindset of the Maestro. A scholarly and practical book that equips the reader's skillsets and competencies for transformational conversations and coaching. A Classic.

—Dr. Keith E. Rolle, The Excellence Network, LLC

Throughout the history of the church, Jesus was known as Prophet, Priest, King, and Friend of Sinners. Dr. Joseph Umidi, in his enlightening book helps us to see that Christ had another title. He was the Master Coach. Through direct and open questions Jesus still coaches us from the gospels.

Jesus, The Master Coach, is an essential book for people who want to fully awake to the dream that God has for their lives, friends, families, and the strangers they meet along the way, and how through asking the right questions we can partner with God in transforming the world.

—Dr. Jeffrey Burns
Consultant for Christian-Muslim Relations
President of Carolina Coastal Coaching

Questions are tools. When used skillfully and at the right time can help you discover gems and nuggets about yourself and God that were formerly hidden in plain sight. As you read *Jesus the Master Coach* you will experience Jesus' adjustments in your life as He uses the tools and wisdom of my friend, Dr. Joseph Umidi.

—David D. Ireland, Ph.D., Lead Pastor & Author
One in Christ; The Kneeling Warrior
www.DavidIreland.org

Contents

Chapter 1
The Questions Behind Our Stories

"...If you knew the gift of God, and who it is that is saying to you, 'Give me a drink,' you would have asked him, and he would have given you living water." John 4:10

WHAT MILESTONE MEMORY, life-altering decision, or "stop-in-your-tracks" direction in your life came as a result of a key question asked in the right way, at the right time, and by the right person?

If you were to interview five to 10 people you admire with the above question you may be amazed to discover or help them find out, that it was a critical question that was the source of their life story journey. It could have been a vocational choice, a behavioral choice, or a marital partner choice, but the final moment source may well have been a question. Maybe it was the ignition to a newly discovered core value passion. Perhaps it was the dynamite that blasted through the tunnel of despair and opened the doorway of hope.

What if we could interview the people on the receiving end of the 100 questions of Jesus in the four gospels? How would their pre- or post-Resurrection stories be based on the moment they heard His question or the months afterward that they reflected on what it meant to them? What if we would follow in His methods and learn how to "ask more and tell less" in our daily interactions?

There's a lot of books written on questions, conversations, connecting, and listening, but there are not many books putting all those together through both the historical Jesus and current stories of real people in complicated situations. I don't know of an approach like this that I've ever seen written. In an unprecedented era of fake news and furious monologues, this perspective is just in time.

1

Over the last 23 years, I've trained over 10,000 people in coaching courses that utilize the principles of this book. The stories that have come back to us over the years have been like burning bushes compelling me to take off my shoes and come aside to pay attention. This book is the result of paying attention long enough to what is working today so that you will make a difference where it matters to you most in your everyday conversations tomorrow.

The Question Behind My Story

I'll never forget the day I walked into a restaurant to chauffeur an individual for a 20-minute drive. I had never met him and was not very interested in getting to know him. I just wanted to drive him, keep the conversation on the surface, and get on with my day. What a shock when he stepped up from his table, put out his hand and said, "Dr. Umidi, I've been looking on your website, and I'd like to ask you a question."

"Of course," I said, thinking that he only wanted to keep the conversation on a superficial level as I did. He only wanted small talk about the history of my area, the weather, or the latest sports game score.

Then he did it. He Asked Up, Listened Up, and Fired Up and made that short conversation matter. Here was the first thing he said:

"Doctor Umidi, if you keep doing in the next five years what you've been doing the last five years, where will you be in making progress toward your big dream and purpose in life?"

I was stunned, like a deer in headlights. Even more stunning was to hear myself respond to a stranger with the truth that only God and I knew.

The truth was that I was not in the right place with myself. I had reached a plateau. Quite frankly, I was boring to myself and others. I was teaching, preaching, and conversing all out of a professional approach that wasn't being real, authentic, or dynamic. I was becoming guilty of the things I despised; corporate spin, religious hype, and small talk. That interchange was my Heart Revealed to me in that exchange.

Somehow, I told him what I just told you. Then 20 minutes later it was over. By the time I delivered him to his destination, he had merely asked me five powerful questions and listened in my response to what mattered to me. The fire in my heart from that interaction caused me to spend the next three months in reflection over what happened that day. That day was the beginning of my heart renewed. I discovered things in this book that I put into practice that caused me to do what he did every day of my life over the last 10 ten years. This book is your proven guide to helping you do that beginning the very first week you read it. You will discover how to Reveal and Renew (R & R) the heart of your family, friends, and fellow citizens in your everyday life.

I asked this individual this question when I met him a year later:

"What happened that day?" I'm good at keeping conversations on the surface. "How did you break through so quickly to my heart and ignite it to live for these kinds of conversations?"

His answer sounded like a line right from Jesus, the Master Coach. "Before I met you, I decided that I unconditionally loved you. I prayed that you would have a breakthrough in this one conversation."

What floored me about his response was that the only person I ever heard of who could unconditionally love me without even knowing me is Jesus himself. The second thing that amazed me was that I did not know that you could be intentional and prepare for a breakthrough conversation and that God would back you up if you used the Master Coach approach!

This book addresses the ordinary conversations in your life; the ones with your kids glued to their technology, your spouse focused on their work, your staff showing up on the outside only, even for yourself not making a living doing what you love. This book focuses on extraordinary results. The result in each chapter is the ignition of hope and passion in the things that matter. After all, the quality of your conversation is a barometer of the quality of those relationships.

This book unashamedly pulls from the great questions asked by Jesus, the master coach. So many of the 100 questions he asked in the four gospels are just in time for us today to be the anecdote to the poisoned and polarized conversations in our cultures. These compelling questions work for everyone because Jesus was the master of being real and not religious. These questions and listening skills work for all times because they carry core values that are needed more than ever. This book will prepare you for conversations that matter because you will be able to do what this man did with me that day in 20 minutes or less... Begin the revelation of God's heart and the revival of your own heart.

> The quality of your conversation is a barometer of the quality of those relationships.

The Question Behind Your Story

Before we get started, let me ask you some questions:

Have you ever heard God questioning you when you were reading the questions He asked others in the four gospels? How about when he asked His disciples, "And who do you say that I am?" How about when he asked Saul, "Why do you persecute Me?" How about when He asked Peter three times, "Do you love me?"

Can I take this to a more intimate level? I promise it will be worth it.

Do you ever ask God questions? Do you sense that He asks you questions? If so, then what question would God ask you today that would light a fire in your heart? What question could you ask God today that would light a fire in his heart?

Maybe we should pause right here and see what will happen from this reflection.

> What question would God ask you today that would
> light a fire in your heart? What question could you
> ask God today that would light a fire in his heart?

Welcome back.

I have discovered that God loves questions. When He came looking for Adam in the garden in the Book of Genesis, He knew his hiding place behind the bush. He knew what he had done to cause him to be aware of his nakedness and shame. Instead of telling, or yelling by declaring, "There you are the first sinner, come out from behind the bushes and fess-up," God started that conversation with this question, "Where are you?" Hope and Passion begin with a God-sized heart expressed in a God-birthed question.

God understands a core way of connecting with us is to give us the freedom to process what we think, what we believe, or what we feel on our own. He knows that ownership of our solutions requires this process. Telling, yelling, or selling may make another get things done on the outside but doesn't allow personal ownership from the inside. God wants us to help others own their responses and honors us in a way that will get us there on our own. His Master Coach method works today more than ever. Here is how it can shape or reshape your story.

Each chapter of this book will unpack the questions that not only made a big difference in the past by the Master but will also make a more significant difference in the present as you follow the Master. We will find it in our homes with parents connecting to their technology-addicted kids. We will discover it in the churches between Boomers and Millennials. We will witness it in our communities or the cultures in our corporations. We can bridge historical differences and rediscover honor that will change the futures for our children's children.

The Question Behind the Stories of Others

Deborah is an amazing woman of God. As a three-decade missionary to Nepal, she has found herself like Harrison Ford in many "Raiders of the Lost Ark" situations, if you can remember that classic movie. The more significant news is that it does not turn off when back in the USA. Whether going shopping or taking the dog for a walk, Deborah does here what she does in Nepal, obeying the voice of God and asking questions like Jesus did and still does.

On Christmas Eve day, 2018 she asked her mailman why he never seems to take a holiday. His answer was simple for him;

"I am not a Christian and don't get all of this materialism at this time of year. What is the meaning of Christmas anyway?"

Deborah knew, at that moment, what you will discover as you read and apply this book. In the few minutes she had before he drove off to the next mail delivery, she would ask him a question that could shape his story into his redemptive adventure.

"Can I tell you the meaning of Christmas right here?" With his permission, she gave a two-minute summary and then ended with this question; "When you get off work today, would you be willing to ask God to reveal to you the real meaning of Christmas? Would you let me know what answer you got the next time I see you?"

The amazing thing is that he said he would. The second amazing thing is that he let Deborah pray for him that he would experience Jesus Christ when he asked. Living like this puts amazing back into grace. It is what questions can ignite daily that gives us all the spirit-led adventure that is our birthright.

Deborah can't wait until she sees him again!

Let's explore the heart of the Master Coach so that you can live this adventure every day. It all begins with getting to the heart of the Master before the technique of asking.

Application Questions

1. What biography or autobiography have you read that reveals a major life change as the result of being asked a key question?

2. Who has asked you a question in your own life story that helped you make a major decision in one direction or another?

3. Who has told you that it was your question asked of them at a key time that made a big difference in the path they chose?

4. What question from Jesus in the gospels comes to mind that made a difference in someone's life?

For FREE additional materials on the topics of
this book please go to this link:

https://lifeforming.net/jmcresources

Chapter 2

Jesus' Questions Reveal the Heart of God

"The heart of the wise teaches his mouth and adds learning to his lips." Proverbs 16:23

Jesus the Master Coach enables any conversation to be a launching pad for transformation.

Cultivating the heart of God comes by abiding in Christ. Powerful conversations come from studying, internalizing, and imitating the way Jesus the Master Coach related to those he encountered, and how he relates to us today.

The coaching heart of God expressed in a great conversation means coming alongside a person as Christ does with us. We want people to experience this same resurrected Christ in our homes, churches, and workplaces so that our communities and cultures will see the heart of God in and through us.

I will never forget the first time that Jesus the Master Coach knocked on my heart's door through a transformational conversation. Pastor Herm Trenholm had guarded his heart the day he got on a ferry boat by asking God to show him who needed a transformational conversation. When he woke up after a quick nap, he noticed that my wife and I were looking out over the ship's rail at the water below.

As he stepped up to the rail, he said, "I always enjoy looking out over the water when I ride this ferry. Sometimes I see schools of fish in these waters on a clear day. Have you seen anything yet?"

"Ah, no. Today is our first time on this boat."

"What are you coming to see on this trip?"

"Well, we are looking to buy some land and live here."

"I can see you are launching a new beginning in your lives."

"Yes, you could say that."

"I can help you see something and someone who could give you the best new beginning you could ever dream of."

Because his heart was ready, he was able to see us with the Father's heart, and then courageously initiated a conversation with us on the boat deck that changed our lives forever. My wife and I came to Christ that glorious day while crossing over from St. John's New Brunswick to Digby, Nova Scotia.

It was not his eloquence. It was the way he saw us and the way he gave us hope to see our lives in a transformational way. That conversation was our launching pad for having this kind of transformational conversation every time we then traveled on that ferry for the next twelve years.

But wait, there is more! Amazingly he coached us monthly for ten years as our spiritual father with the heart of a coach, mostly by written letters! On the celebration of his 50 years in the ministry, my wife and I flew back to Nova Scotia for what we thought was a small family gathering. There, in an old lobster hall building, were 135 couples that he had led to the Lord and coached with the same heart! Jesus, the Master Coach, had used this humble man of God to launch transformation in all of these couples that were now serving the Lord with the same heart.

The questions and conversations of Jesus always see people in terms of destiny.

The coaching heart of God looks at people from God's point of view, in terms of their destiny. We want to instinctively tune into their God-given capacity, their untapped potential, and watch for the fleeting glimpses of the image of God in them, and then consistently relate to individuals in those terms. By seeing people in this way, we help them understand themselves in new ways, and that opens the door to transformation.

My granddaughter is my heroine. Born with Spinal Muscular Atrophy (SMA) she has been in her wheelchair since she was five years old. Now, at 27, we still believe God will raise her out of that chair, but if not, she still has a destiny in that chair and a life message through that chair.

Things got complicated when she got diabetes and then cyclical vomiting syndrome. In 2016, she was in ER 33 times, several with life-threatening ketosis and most of the time with an inability to get an IV in her. As her grandfather and as the head of a coach training movement in 31 countries and 15 languages I knew that she did not see herself in terms of her destiny, but that I could.

As I sat in front of my laptop crying out to God to help me to see her as He does, Jesus showed up and enabled me to write with tears of inspiration. I described a good week in the life of my granddaughter while she was still in her chair but without the ER trips. I did not make it up but strung together the brief and infrequent conversations I was able to have with her when she was lucid that painful year. Here is an excerpt from it:

Unique Design

Jessica is a people person. Good friendships, fun, and conversations energize her. She is a person people like to be around. She is attractive in multiple ways and very engaging as a young adult who can weigh in on any conversation

Jessica is a creative person. She has an eye for artistry in several venues and knows what is compelling to the eye and design.

Jessica is an adventurous person. She loves to be on the move and has an explorer ability to experience changing environments.

Unique Desires

Jessica is genuine. She lives and breathes for authenticity and real friendship.

Jessica is a developer. She loves to develop people in their growth and potential.

Jessica is a motivator. She models a can-do attitude in the midst of circumstances beyond one's control.

Unique Dreams

Jessica envisions teaching, training, and influencing children to shape their futures.

Jessica sees herself helping those in influential public roles to project their best by her professional ability as a "make-up artist."

Jessica projects herself as a compelling and informative tour guide for the New York City market in museums, special needs children camps, and specialty restaurants.

Unique Destiny

Jessica is destined to leave a winner's legacy that will give courage and hope to many through her success and her unique story in her adult life. She will inspire.

Unique Story

By 2022, Jessica has the joy of managing her busy schedule. Her typical week involves her blog and articles she writes from her studio apartment in NYC. Many of her responses are to the people who were impacted by her personally and professionally during one of the tours she led. Several museums have hired her two nights a week and one weekend a month.

Jessica enjoys her weekly preparations for the classes she teaches to the international elementary school children that she can get to on her own from her apartment. Because of her impact on these children, Jessica takes two trips a year to visit them in their home countries for both her personal learning and her ongoing continuing education as a part-time teacher and tutor for them. Her presence in these cultures has inspired others who have not dreamed of possibilities like this in their lives.

Jessica is managing regular invitations to appear on TV and radio for help in fundraising for special-needs children. One of the joys she has found through this service is that she has met numerous well-known celebrities and leaders, several of which have hired her to be their make-up artist when in town for various functions.

Jessica finds her restoration and rests in hosting her numerous friends from all over the globe who come to NYC with theater attendance, gourmet restaurants, and even in her dinner parties in which she has become somewhat of a celebrity cook in her circles. Her favorite time of year is the summer when she travels to several camps as a counselor for special needs children; especially enjoying the fishing outings that she leads as both a tour guide and an expert fisherman.

By 2022, Jessica is sought out for her consulting advice to empower special-needs families and organizations in such areas as arts and entertainment, outdoor sports, and cooking. She has even helped others in the launch of a cooking channel that specializes in people with unique needs. She has a waiting list of clients who pay her top rates as a life coach to help them maximize their lives no matter what.

When she read this letter, she wept. Hope arose in her, and she knew that God, I, and others saw her in terms of her destiny now so that she could believe it was coming to her when she was able to enjoy it and steward it. The great news is that she is now living that out while in her chair; and even better, she is helping others see themselves in terms of their destiny.

When we start to interact at home, work, church, and community consistently with the heart of Jesus the Master Coach we find out what we are capable of, and surprisingly, so will others. When that discipline has fully molded us, it becomes a powerful channel where the heart of a coach can reach-out to touch and transform everyone within our sphere of influence.

"Who do men say that I am?"

The question for any serious follower of Jesus the Master Coach begins with this; "Why haven't I heard this before?" I know about Jesus, the Teacher, Jesus, the Prophet, Jesus, the Healer, Jesus, the Evangelist, Jesus, the Suffering Servant. How could I have missed Jesus, the Master Coach?

Understood. It is like the Trinity. We can't find that word in the scriptures, but we have overwhelming evidence that it is a major doctrine of our orthodoxy.

Most of my formation, discipleship, leadership, and ministry training focused on the teaching of Jesus with very little on the questions of Jesus. That is why most of my life I have focused on teaching rather than questioning. My goal was world-class ability at monologues while having third-world development on dialogues. When God opened my eyes, I saw that dialogues, not monologues make disciples. My students had miles of notes and quotes but inches of transformational conversations.

> When God opened my eyes, I saw that disciples are made by dialogues, not monologues. My students had miles of notes and quotes but inches of transformational conversations.

How much time would it take you today to sit down and read everything that the Holy Spirit gave us in the teachings of Jesus in the scriptures so that we could become maturing disciples and multiplying leaders? Without reading the duplications in the four gospels, you could do it in 45 minutes!

When we open our eyes to the questions of Jesus, we see that much of the identity, values, heart, mindset, and vision that Jesus forms in the first disciples, and still, forms in us come from what those questions do when we engage God with them.

Because we have skipped over the 100 Questions of Jesus in the New Testament, we have missed a key to sustainable transformation, accelerated discipleship, and penetrating kingdom influence in our daily lives. We have majored on the content of the Master Teacher without paying enough attention to the actual pedagogy of the Master Coach.

> We have majored on the content of the Master Teacher without paying enough attention to the actual pedagogy of the Master Coach.

One of our schools' Ph.D. graduates spent years on the mission field making disciples and leaders who made disciples and leaders according to 2 Timothy 2:2. "And the things that you have heard from me among many witnesses, commit these to faithful men who will be able to teach others also"

When he analyzed the time management of Jesus' disciple-making efforts, he concluded that Jesus spent less time delivering content and more time on stewarding the context. He found that this was not optional for a church planting movement missional paradigm. It was and still is the intentional plan of Jesus the Master Coach to disciple a nation versus nurture a denominational institution.

Here is the summary of how he describes it:
- Instruction (Content) = Teaching/Training
- Relationships (Context) = Coach/Mentor Conversations
- Experiences (Context) = Application/Questions/Reflection
- God Encounters (Context) = Engaging God in daily dialogues

Here is a way that I like to communicate his research. We need all four quadrants operating in our lives to become like Jesus the Master Coach. We also need to emphasize what Jesus did; more context informed by content rather than more content illustrated by context.

1. Life-forming Content = God's Word
2. Life-changing Relationships = Coaching Conversations
3. Life-stretching Experiences = Application/Questions/Reflection
4. Life-altering God Encounters = Supernatural divine appointments

The genius of the Jesus method is that transformation comes from any combination of the above that includes the Word of God. This is the foundation for the Holy Spirit to do His primary work of "bringing all things to remembrance" regarding the Word of God (content) informing the mission of God (context).

> But the Helper, the Holy Spirit, whom the Father will send in My name, He will teach you all things, and bring to your **remembrance** all things that I said to you.
>
> John 14:26

The incredible power of the context, which focuses on the crucial role of questions, reflection, de-brief, and feedback, is that it brings to heart and mind the content which can interpret it. I call it the "This is that" or the "This is what" of God.

> [14] But Peter, standing up with the eleven, raised his voice and said to them, "Men of Judea and all who dwell in Jerusalem, let this be known to you, and heed my words.
>
> [15] For these are not drunk, as you suppose, since it is only the third hour of the day.
>
> [16] But this is what was spoken by the prophet Joel:
>
> [17] 'And it shall come to pass in the last days, says God, That I will pour out of My Spirit on all flesh; Your sons and your daughters shall prophesy, Your young men shall see visions, Your old men shall dream dreams.
>
> [18] 'And on My menservants and on My maidservants I will pour out My Spirit in those days; and they shall prophesy.
>
> [19] 'I will show wonders in heaven above and signs in the earth beneath: Blood and fire and vapor of smoke.

²⁰ 'The sun shall be turned into darkness, and the moon into blood, before the coming of the great and awesome day of the Lord.

²¹ 'And it shall come to pass that whoever calls on the name of the Lord shall be saved.'"

Acts 2:14-21

Are you sensing your heart is getting "strangely warmed," maybe even enlarged for the role of the questions of Jesus in and through your life?

If questions are the key to revealing the heart of God, how might they be the key to revealing the heart of us? I believe that the difference between a whole-hearted disciple and a half-hearted disciple is ignited by questions; those we are asked and those we discover how to ask. I promise you it will blast the boredom in your Christian walk, ruin you for merely settling for a meeting event mentality, and silence the border bullies that have hemmed you into a limited corner in our culture. This following chapter may be just in time for the call of God through you for such a time as this!

> I believe that the difference between a whole-hearted disciple and a half-hearted disciple is ignited by questions; those we are asked and those we discover how to ask.

Application Questions

1. What percentage of your spiritual development or discipleship experience in your church background has been through monologue? What percentage has been through dialogue? If we reversed these percentages, what difference might that have made to where you are today?

2. Who has modeled the heart of God to you in the questions they asked you, including the way they asked them?

3. Who has not modeled the heart of God to you in the way they asked you questions?

4. What do you most need to learn from this chapter to influence the significant people in your life?

For FREE additional materials on the topics of
this book please go to this link:

https://lifeforming.net/jmcresources

Chapter 3

Jesus' Questions
Reveal our Heart

"...Out of the Abundance of the Heart the mouth speaks."
Matthew 12:34

CAN YOU ENVISION an important conversation you need to have with someone that matters in the near future? What would be a wonderful outcome, a major breakthrough, a great resolution for that conversation? What would be a disappointment, a setback, a breakdown from that conversation? If your preferred future from that conversation is a breakthrough instead of a breakdown, then we need a heart-check before we do a spell-check.

Before people are reading our lips, they're reading our heart. They're picking up on our attitudes, our spirit, our perspective on them. There's a big difference between a childlike curiosity in our questions and a "here comes the judge and jury" attitude that people will pick up before we even say a word.

> Keep your heart with all vigilance, for from it flow the springs of life.
>
> Proverbs 4:23

If your preferred future from that conversation is a breakthrough instead of a breakdown, then we need a heart-check before we do a spell-check.

We are surrounded by all kinds of tools and aids to guard our homes, our identities, our intellectual properties, our passwords, and anything else we deem important to us. Yet we are unguarded and unprotected at the heart level; the wellspring and source of life-giving interactions that define our lives.

Here are seven core pieces of equipment that will guard your heart as you prepare to face your next important conversation. One or more of them may be the key to creating a milestone moment and memory. Make sure they fit you and your situation but do not leave home without them!

Number 1: Believing in people.

Like Jesus' belief in us, the unconditional belief in another unleashes the power of God for change in their life.

> From now on, therefore, we regard no one according to the flesh.
> Even though we once regarded Christ according to the flesh, we
> regard him thus no longer. Therefore, if anyone is in Christ, he is a
> new creation. The old has passed away; behold, the new has come.
> 2 Corinthians 5:16-17

This means believing in them, even when they hardly believe in themselves. The First step up of a breakthrough conversation is stepping into a larger belief in the person you are talking to and a larger outcome that you both want to achieve from that conversation. No matter what you ask, when you ask, or where you ask, it's how you ask from a position of belief that can make your day and their day; and that, my friend, will make all the difference.

My wife is the most amazing person with so many qualities that I admire. It took her years to believe the statement I just made.

As a first-grader, she was accomplished in music and had grade-school and high-school events that showcased her voice and talent. Not once did her hard-working parents attend any of these. Not once did her father ever affirm her. When I met her at a theater production in which she was the main actor and singer, I was amazed at her talent and spirit. As I got to know her, I was perplexed by how little she believed in herself. I had no problem believing in her, but it took her years to believe that the person I loved could receive it as truth.

Quick question: Can you think of a question that Jesus asked out of the 100 we have found in the New Testament that communicated believing in people? Try this one as an example:

> When Jesus had raised Himself up and saw no one but the woman, He said to her, "Woman, where are those accusers of yours? Has no one condemned you?"
>
> She said, "No one, Lord."
>
> And Jesus said to her, "Neither do I condemn you; go and sin no more."
>
> John 8:10-11

Think about your typical week. How often have you asked questions that communicate believing in the other person? For those times you missed the opportunity, how could you have stepped up first to prepare yourself to believe in the other person in a breakthrough way?

Too many times I've come home from work wishing I had stepped up first into my action-hero suit before disciplining my kids. Those memorable times that I parked the car and stepped into the best version of myself were the ones in which even the discipline of my son delivered a breakthrough.

Here is the challenge. It seems easy to believe in people before you really get to know them. What if the more you get to know them and realize their glaring limitations that the end result is seeing more of the limitations than what they actually are or could become? Those are the times when I intentionally remind myself of how I first saw them, encountered them, and believed in them. That exercise of remembrance will reset our focus, enabling the reset of our belief system. That small shift of belief in the person will help them become the best version of themselves as well.

Number 2: Engage them where God is at work.

God is the sovereign initiator of our growth, setting the agenda and motivating us to grow through the real events in our lives. Change starts with God's action.

> Then Jesus answered and said to them, "Most assuredly, I say to you, the Son can do nothing of Himself, but what He sees the Father do; for whatever He does, the Son also does in like manner."
>
> John 5:19

Of all the changes someone might feel obligated to be working on, or you think they should be working on, where are they most energized to make those changes, and where is that motivation coming from? When God initiates change in us, He sustains it with an ongoing conviction, an ongoing vision, and ongoing energy to accomplish it.

> "for it is God who works in you, both to will and to work for His good pleasure."
>
> Philippians 2:13

That's the best place to add our belief and our energy in any conversation with someone.

When God initiates change in us, He sustains it with an ongoing conviction, an ongoing vision, and ongoing energy to accomplish it.

Jack and I used to drive the 40 miles each day to the seminary we attended in Nova Scotia. There were so many conversations I had with him about all the things I needed to change in my life. After dropping out of law school, I was in a mindset of living day to day, confused about life, vocation, money, family, and how to be a better father and husband. I could have had a transactional conversational agenda for every trip if it was just up to me.

Jack somehow found a way to make those road trips transformational. I did not know it then, but his questions were revealing his heart to work with what was most important in my life at that time. As we drove past the apple orchards in the Annapolis Valley in the late fall that still had unpicked rotting apples clinging, it reminded me of all the bad fruit that I needed to deal with in my life. Jack's questions and conversations became like the spring sap flowing in those trees that would cause the old apples to fall away on their own as the new began to blossom.

Henry Blackaby's wonderful book, *Experiencing God*, was a milestone for many of us to simply find out where the Holy Spirit is moving and partner with him in that. So much of the fruit that remains, so much of the sustainable change comes by first stepping up into a place of seeing where God is at work, and then and only then, adding our work to that in any conversation and relationship.

I will never forget the couples who came to me for marriage counseling only wanting to focus on the changes they demanded from their spouse. When I refused to begin on that agenda, they almost walked out. Amazingly, it was when we all discovered that God was focusing on their weekly caring behaviors, that they recovered their caring feelings for each other and found the energy to change the irritating behaviors.

Number 3: Leader/adults take stewardship responsibility for their own growth and development.

Taking responsibility for others stunts their growth.

> But solid food belongs to those who are of full age, that is, those who by reason of use have their senses exercised to discern both good and evil.
>
> Hebrews 5:14

That means we don't have to be Mr. or Mrs. Fix-it in any conversation, even if we have the answers for every one of their situations. Helping people to exercise their own thinking, research, and even baby-step initiative levels will cause them to accelerate their own growth. They will learn to lift the heavier weights later when there's no one else around but them. Personal Leadership Effectiveness is when people stop demanding entitlement service and are able to govern themselves and take the steering wheel of their heart and dreams for their own future.

I have had to learn the hard way that the number-one killer of authentic relationships is giving advice that no one is asking for. My wake-up call came when I realized that there was little guarantee that what worked for me would work for you because there were so many differences in each of our contexts that it is far wiser to consider you the expert in your domain than me.

I have had to learn the hard way that the number-one killer of authentic relationships is giving advice that no one is asking for.

I believe in the healing power of prayer through the resurrected Christ and have seen God work wonders many times. I have never seen my granddaughter come out of her wheelchair and be healed from her Spinal Muscular Atrophy condition even though I and many others have prayed over her in the last fifteen years.

I know what some of you are thinking as you read this. If only you prayed this way or if only you declared over her in this manner, or… That is what happens to me whenever I share this story publicly. Inevitably, I have one or a few who want to tell me what worked for them and why they are convinced it will work for me. I understand how important it is for them to try to help, so I listen. Inside, however, I hear myself saying that I did not ask for that advice and I probably would not be interested in an authentic relationship with the one who just gave it.

Number 4: Recognize that transformation is primarily experiential and relational, not informational.

The things that most deeply shape us happen through experiences and relationships, not by accumulating information. Therefore, Jesus the Master Coach in us focuses on engaging the teachable moments of life in the context of a transparent relationship to produce lasting change.

> I have heard of You by the hearing of the ear. But now my eye
> sees You.
>
> Job 42:5

That means we don't need to be sage on the stage with infomercials in our conversations. With interactions that create meaningful reflection and debrief, any conversation can connect the battery cables to jumpstart real transformation in the minds of those we care about.

I had an addiction to overwhelming my clients or students with additional handouts and resources with the initial misconception that "transformation comes from more information." I even announced in my classes in graduate school, *"You can make an appointment and come up and copy anything you want from my files that would be of help to you."* I became king of the information mountain to my students, but the end result was that I kept them in the base camp of the transformation mountain. "Just google it" will not result in transformation any more than "just copy it" did from my files.

Number 5: Authenticity is the key to trust.

Transparent relationships free us from secret sins and hidden fears that tie us down and give God access to our lives in a deeper way. The key is in our hands to intentionally foster an authentic atmosphere. When we turn that key in a conversation there is a new openness to God and others that comes rushing in like a light in a dark room.

> O Corinthians! We have spoken openly to you; our heart is wide open. You are not restricted by us, but you are restricted by your own affections. Now in return for the same (I speak as to children), you also be open.
>
> 2 Corinthians 6:11-13

In my first pastoral experience, we invited two singles to spend a couple of days in the parsonage that had many rooms. Little did we know that they were secretly sleeping together. In the presence of God, in a powerful prayer meeting with them on the third day, they came clean and repented. It happened when we were authentic with them about being concerned with another issue of trust we were having. Our authentic voicing of one area allowed them to be real with us in this critical area.

For a conversation to be authentic, we must step up and go first by initiating it. When we step up first, we can catalyze it by giving people permission to go there as well if they choose.

I deal with corporate politics and ambitions, and I am fully aware that some things are better pondered in the heart than shared from our mouths. Some of the toxic work cultures I experienced in the non-profit and for-profit world count it as a sign of weakness to be authentic. When you walk in their doors, you put on your "fake it till you make it face." At the end of the day, it is a matter of becoming secure in your own skin and recognizing that your identity is not determined by your image. "He was getting to be more real than religious" is my hoped-for inscription on my tombstone. Maybe it will change the conversations at the gravesite!

> At the end of the day, it is a matter of becoming secure in your own skin and recognizing that your identity is not determined by your image.

Number 6: Each person is unique.

Through the eyes of Jesus, we can see them as a uniquely valuable individual with a distinctive gifting, history, and call.

> If the whole body were an eye, where would be the hearing? If the whole were hearing, where would be the smelling? But now God has set the members, each one of them, in the body just as He pleased. And if they were all one member, where would the body be?
>
> 1 Corinthians 12:17-19

That means we need to help them celebrate their uniqueness and not simply tolerate it. By stepping up to honor them and naming their unique design, we give them the gift of being seen, known, and prized.

I have trained over 1,700 staff at one of the fastest growing universities in the U.S. with one of the highest retention rates. Though I was part of other great initiatives to see this amazing accomplishment, my main role was to be sure that every staff member took every opportunity to discover and celebrate every student's uniqueness. At the top of our profile of a retained student is the phrase, "I am known."

I show them a YouTube monologue called "The Woman at the Well." It is a powerful presentation in which she keeps repeating this phrase, "To be known is to be loved, and to be loved is to be known." The transformational power of being known in our uniqueness has taken root in our university staff. That is one reason our student retention rate is in the low 90-percentile. It is the difference between being a number or being a name.

> To him the doorkeeper opens, and the sheep hear his voice; and he calls his own sheep by name and leads them out.
>
> John 10:3

That means that every staff steps up before they go to work to be ready to have a conversation that moves a student from a "number identity" to a "family identity." To be known is to be loved and to be loved is to be known.

Number 7: We can see and respond to people the way our heavenly father does.

That means an increase in our unconditional love tank, at least moving up 15-40% higher, is possible and doable for all of us. That's what I experienced that day in that 20-minute drive. This man stepped up first before he asked up second, and when he stepped into unconditional love the heart of God through his heart softened my heart and gave me hope again that I could become the best version of myself.

Without affirmative action programs and hiring personnel to attract diverse students, we now enjoy, as of this writing, a minority of our student population coming from the majority ethnicity population...in a student body that has now exceeded 11,000. The number-one reason given by our esteemed founder and president of our 40-year young university is simple; "We just want our students to know the love we have for them and for their futures." Simply profound. Simply irresistible.

Now that we laid out the heart of stepping up to be the best version of yourself, it is time for you to find your "just in time" chapter for your next big conversation. In fact, we have an acronym that can put all of this into an "easy-peasy" way of making this work where you live and work. Welcome to the DOOR into your new and improved interactions!

Application Questions

1. Think about your typical week. How often have you asked questions that communicate believing in the other person? For those times you missed the opportunity, how could you have stepped up first to prepare yourself to believe in the other person in a breakthrough way?

2. How do you sense God is nudging, prodding, convicting, energizing, or leading you to grow or develop in a new area? How can you be more intentional in looking to help another person see that and pursue that in themselves?

3. Where or with whom do you tend to be an advice giver, without even thinking about whether that is what they are asking for? How can you become more self-aware and self-managed in that default behavior?

4. Which of these seven core pieces of equipment are you focusing on to guard your heart in this season of your life?

For FREE additional materials on the topics of this book please go to this link:

https://lifeforming.net/jmcresources

Chapter 4

Jesus' Questions Open a D.O.O.R. to Other Hearts

"Behold, I stand at the door and knock. If anyone hears My voice and opens the door, I will come in to him and dine with him, and he with Me." Revelation 3:20

MANY TIMES, HEARING THE VOICE of Jesus the Master Coach is hearing the questions of Jesus. We can categorize those questions into an acronym that helps us to identify the type of question He asks then and now. It is also a helpful model on the kind of questions Jesus can ask through us to others.

CATEGORY ONE in the D.O.O.R. model is "D" that identifies Direct questions.

Direct questions point straight to the heart of the topic without beating around the bush. This is how "straight shooters" interact with people. They go right for the jugular early and often and consider it a waste of their interactive time if they do not get there in any conversation. Jesus knew when and how to be direct and modeled for us the master way to be direct with the right question for the right context.

For instance, Jesus was not demonstrating His Master Coach methodology when he was directly confronting those who were plotting to trip him, shut Him down, or kill him. In His "Woe to you..." statements in the book of Matthew, Chapter 23, it is clear that the conversations He would have with those who would use any and every question in a diabolical manner would not be the same type of directness we would use with a friend or team member. Antagonists are not seeking a conversation but annihilation, and sometimes silence is the best response.

All over the world when I ask an audience to shout out the first question of Jesus that comes to mind the one I hear over 80% of the time is *"Who do you say that I am?"* That direct question has stood out in minds of people from every tribe and nation perhaps because of the spectacular results in the response of Peter when he said, *"Thou Art the Christ, the son of the Living God."*

Antagonists are not seeking a conversation but annihilation, and sometimes silence is the best response.

Since Jesus the Master Coach has an intentional pedagogy about His use of questions for us in making disciples, we can reintroduce some underemphasized principles back into our churches and spiritual formation by looking more closely at His questions. Here is one: *Some Revelation only comes on the other side of a powerful question.*

Some Revelation only comes on the other side of a powerful question.

Let's take a closer look at the context of this passage to see more insights on the role of questions that bring revelation (illumination is more theologically correct):

> When Jesus came into the region of Caesarea Philippi He asked His disciples, saying, *"Who do men say that I, the Son of Man, am?"*[A] So they said, "Some *say* John the Baptist, some Elijah, and others Jeremiah or one of the prophets."

[A] Beginning with third person before first person, "Who do men...?" is a core way to help clients process their own understanding without having to own their own response; ("Some say...others..." v.14). Direct questions too soon may put people on the defensive, but third person questions can disarm their defensiveness.

He said to them, "But who do you say that I am?"ᴮ

Simon Peter answered and said, "You are the Christ, the Son of the living God."

Jesus answered and said to him, "Blessed are you, Simon Bar-Jonah, for flesh and blood has not revealedᶜ this to you, but My Father who is in heaven."

Matthew 16:13-17

Perhaps some of us need to step up our game to be more direct in our questions and less indirect? I can remember a time in my life when I would be supervising someone and trying to correct them; however, my conversation and my questions were so indirect that the person left my office thinking that I was actually encouraging them in the same behavior that I meant to correct!

I was coaching a wonderful teacher in an Asian training academy when she told me how her directness in her questioning and conversation was getting her in trouble with her manager. It seemed like all the other employees were cheering her on to be the spokesperson for employee concerns, and the more she did it, the more she found herself being "brutally honest" in her questions and interactions. She was waiting for me to chastise her or correct her when I simply asked her this question; *"How might you move to a better version of yourself by keeping your strength of being direct yet choosing to become more "disarmingly honest" and eliminating the brutal edge?"*

Something special happened to her at that moment. She saw intuitively that the direct questions of Jesus the Master Coach were meant to disarm tensions rather than start an arms race between people or groups. The guilt, shame, and condemnation rolled off her as she realized she could celebrate who she is with a new identity by simply changing the adjective that went with her style of questions.

Here are some examples of direct questions that can and should be used in our everyday relationships:

"How do you think God intends for you to handle the situation?"

"In what way is that decision going to take you where you want to go?"

ᴮ Here is the direct, first-person question that requires a clear, owned, personal response. Because Jesus did not lead with this, He gave room for personal Reflection and cultural Relating to others, a key to the process of breakthrough illumination.

ᶜ Core Coaching Principle: Some revelation will only come on the other side of a powerful question asked in the right way, at the right time, and in the right place.

One caution with the use of direct questions is that sometimes they can withdraw from the relational bank account of trust and acceptance of the other person in a conversation.

That means it is best to have deposited into the other person a series of conversational affirmations so that our direct questions have something left over to withdraw from. Being direct too soon, if you have not built a bank account of relational equity with someone ahead of time, may shut them down and even result in others getting defensive.

Remember this principle: Following the conversational heart and methods of Jesus the Master Coach will mean dying to yourself so that others may come to life. That means denying your natural born propensity to be automatically direct by default in your questions while finding the best way to connect with the person in a way they can best receive your questions. In the D.O.O.R. model, that may mean leading more with the next category of questions instead of what you may normally do by leading with the direct approach up front.

> Following the conversational heart and methods of
> Jesus the Master Coach will mean dying to yourself
> so that others may come to life.

CATEGORY TWO in the D.O.O.R. model is "O" that identifies Open questions.

(*Examples:* "*Could you tell me a little more about that?*" "*What was significant to you about that experience?*")

Open questions open the door to an area of conversation but let the other person decide if they want to go through that door. By opening the door, we give them permission to go through if they choose, but we do not force them to do so if they are not willing or ready.

The difference between open and closed questions is that typically a closed question is answered with yes, no, or I don't know. This is especially true with our adolescent children at meal times! An open question causes people to be able to process, to reflect, and to give more detail. The more powerful an open question fits the context the more likely the other will stop talking on auto-pilot and take the steering wheel of their heart in a genuine response to our question.

The more powerful an open question fits the context the more likely the other will stop talking on auto-pilot and take the steering wheel of their heart in a genuine response to our question.

In Luke 24, Jesus asked the two confused disciples on the Emmaus road a **penetrating open question** that set them up for a breakthrough.

> [13] Now behold, two of them were traveling that same day to a village called Emmaus, which was seven miles from Jerusalem. [14] And they talked together of all these things which had happened. [15] So it was, while they conversed and reasoned,[D] that Jesus Himself drew near and went with them.[E] [16] But their eyes were restrained, so that they did not know Him.[F]
>
> [17] And He said to them, "What kind of conversation *is* this that you have with one another as you walk and are sad?"[G]
>
> [18] Then the one whose name was Cleopas answered and said to Him, "Are You the only stranger in Jerusalem, and have You not known the things which happened there in these days?"
>
> [19] And He said to them, "What things?"[H]
>
> So they said to Him, "The things concerning Jesus of Nazareth, who was a Prophet mighty in deed and word before God and all the people, [20] and how the chief priests and our rulers delivered Him to be condemned to death, and crucified Him.

[D] "Reasoned" implies that both their "self-talk" and interchange was rational, logical, and circular in their assumptions and reinforced the "group think" in their circles.

[E] The *first coaching posture* is to be "fully present" and "be with" another in their walk to build trust.

[F] Coaching questions are more intuitive than rational and can "disrupt" the blind spots of others who are not "seeing" through the circumstances beyond their control.

[G] The *second coaching posture* is to ask powerful and penetrating questions that causes reflection and deep ownership of the another's responses. SEE APPENDIX for "Conversational Champion" certification.

[H] Indicates a probing question in the OPS model (Observing, Probing, Sifting taught in the ACT Coaching Course).

[21] But we were hoping[I] that it was He who was going to redeem Israel. Indeed, besides all this, today is the third day since these things happened. [22] Yes, and certain women of our company, who arrived at the tomb early, astonished us. [23] When they did not find His body, they came saying that they had also seen a vision of angels who said He was alive. [24] And certain of those *who were* with us went to the tomb and found *it* just as the women had said; but Him they did not see."

[25] Then He said to them, "O foolish ones, and slow of heart to believe[J] in all that the prophets have spoken! [26] Ought not the Christ to have suffered these things and to enter into His glory?" [27] And beginning at Moses and all the Prophets, He expounded to them in all the Scriptures the things concerning Himself.

[28] Then they drew near to the village where they were going, and He indicated that He would have gone farther. [29] But they constrained Him, saying, "Abide with us, for it is toward evening, and the day is far spent." And He went in to stay with them.

[30] Now it came to pass, as He sat at the table with them, that He took bread, blessed and broke *it,* and gave it to them. [31] Then their eyes were opened[K] and they knew Him; and He vanished from their sight.

[32] And they said to one another, "Did not our heart burn within us while He talked with us on the road,[L] and while He opened the Scriptures to us?" [33] So they rose up that very hour and returned to Jerusalem, and found the eleven and those *who were* with them

---

[I] The *third coaching posture* is to Listen to What Really Matters…in this case the loss of hope.

[J] The *fourth coaching posture* is to Authentically speak the truth in love to another. "Slow of heart" (*katartismos* in Greek) demonstrates a hard heart issue, perhaps referencing the common dilemma of others who are locked into a specific interpretation of their dreams to be fulfilled, thereby experiencing disillusionment and deep disappointment when it does not happen.

[K] Though not with the 12 in the Upper Room for the Last Supper, the way Jesus broke the bread could have been key to their illumination. This indicates the role of visual and metaphor to capture hearts and imaginations in others, many times more powerful than words themselves.

[L] Here is a key to coaching transformation; "strangely warmed" or burning hearts! Notice that this came from both the conversation only, AND the bible study given by Jesus Himself. Coaching can ignite hearts without bible chapter and verse references which will encourage a coaching movement in the marketplace.

gathered together, ³⁴ saying, "The Lord is risen indeed, and has appeared to Simon!" ³⁵ And they told about the things *that had happened* on the road,ᴹ and how He was known to them in the breaking of bread.

³⁶ Now as they said these things, Jesus Himself stood in the midst of them, and said to them, "Peace to you." ³⁷ But they were terrified and frightened, and supposed they had seen a spirit. ³⁸ And He said to them, "Why are you troubled? And why do doubts arise in your hearts? ³⁹ Behold My hands and My feet, that it is I Myself. Handle Me and see, for a spirit does not have flesh and bones as you see I have."

⁴⁰ When He had said this, He showed them His hands and His feet. ⁴¹ But while they still did not believe for joy, and marveled, He said to them, "Have you any food here?" ⁴² So they gave Him a piece of a broiled fish and some honeycomb. ⁴³ And He took *it* and ate in their presence.

⁴⁴ Then He said to them, "These *are* the words which I spoke to you while I was still with you, that all things must be fulfilled which were written in the Law of Moses and *the* Prophets and *the* Psalms concerning Me." ⁴⁵ And He opened their understanding, that they might comprehend the Scriptures.

⁴⁶ Then He said to them, "Thus it is written, and thus it was necessary for the Christ to suffer and to rise from the dead the third day, ⁴⁷ and that repentance and remission of sins should be preached in His name to all nations, beginning at Jerusalem. ⁴⁸ And you are witnesses of these things. ⁴⁹ Behold, I send the Promise of My Father upon you; but tarry in the city of Jerusalem until you are endued with power from on high."

Luke 24:13-49

What would Jesus ask through you on your Emmaus road this week?

What if we had an app that could track our conversations on the roads we take each week? Here is what this chapter could do for you while we are waiting for that innovation:

ᴹ The "currency of the Kingdom" is Relationships. The "currency of relationships" is Conversations.

Simply *Ask More and Tell Less*. With intentionality, smart goals, and peer accountability, we can actually do conversation management like we do time management in our lives. Here is one way to do it:

TELLING — ASKING — DIRECT — OPEN — CLOSED

We could have a buddy listen to us as we step up into a conversation and track every time we chose one of the categories above. We could record our conversation and then play it back and score ourselves. We could create a competitive game with a team to see how many conversations they could listen to and how many times those resulted in score sheets with winners finding the most times questions were used and what kind were most used.

> With intentionality, smart goals, and peer accountability, we can actually do conversation management like we do time management in our lives.

After I explain to my college students in any of my classes that I am teaching how to get an "A" at the first class, I then spring my surprise on them. It sounds something like this each semester:

"Here is how I want you to integrate your student life into your everyday life. Each week between classes, look for an opportunity to step into a conversation and see how asking open and direct questions can make a difference. Especially listen for opportunities to shift the complaining and confusion tone, and see if your questions can bring a new perspective that would not have happened had you not stepped up and asked up. This is your Emmaus road assignment each week that won't get you an 'A' in the class but will get you an 'A' in your influence. Oh, by the way, I will also be doing this with you, expecting a story to tell each week when we meet."

The next week, I am the only one who made the attempt. By the third week, I have two to three stories from others. By the seventh week, everyone is eager to share their story. From then on, it is standing room only each semester as enrolled students want to invite their friends to hear the stories that take place in this first 10 minutes of each class time. It happens without fail every time because the resurrected Jesus the Master Coach is still on the Emmaus road through us when we wake up fully to the harvest and have our eyes wide open to the mercies of God that are new every morning!

Application Questions

1. On a scale of 1-10 with 10 being extremely direct and one being extremely indirect, where do you typically land? What insight has this chapter given you to be more intentional about making a shift in that percentage?

2. How did the explanation of the Matthew 16 passage open up your understanding of the power of this statement: "Some revelation will only come on the other side of a powerful question"?

3. How did the notes on the Luke 24 passage give you a picture of your own Emmaus road opportunities in your everyday life?

4. How might the information on "Conversational Champion" described in the Appendix apply to your church or organization?

For FREE additional materials on the topics of
this book please go to this link:

https://lifeforming.net/jmcresources

Chapter 5

Jesus' Questions Open a D.O.O.R. to Other Hearts (Part 2)

"Behold, I stand at the door and knock. If anyone hears My voice and opens the door, I will come in to him and dine with him, and he with Me." Revelation 3:20

JESUS THE MASTER COACH is asking us today the same question He asked the Emmaus road disciples in Luke 24:17.

> And He said to them, "What kind of conversation is this that you have with one another as you walk and are sad?"

The Master of Conversations knows what amateur conversations are about. That is why He asks us what kind we are having each day. That is why I ask all my students what their conversations are like outside the classroom.

Through the D.O.O.R. model we are finally able to move beyond small talk, shop talk, sports talk, busy talk, idle talk, and group-thinking, circular talk into a deeper, meaningful, Real Talk that is creative and powerful. It even can give us hope when our interpretations of how things would work out did not meet our expectations.

> The Master of Conversations knows what amateur conversations are about. That is why He asks us what kind we are having each day.

But we were hoping that it was He who was going to redeem Israel...

Luke 24:21

From there I will give back her vineyards to her, and turn the "Valley of Trouble" into an "Opportunity for Hope." There she will sing as she did when she was young, when she came up from the land of Egypt.

Hosea 2:15

The key to the closed hearts and locked doors in our polarized monologues today is conversations that bring all the parts of the Master Coach D.O.O.R. acronym which will result in transformational dialogues. Let's unpack the last two parts of this model.

CATEGORY THREE in the D.O.O.R. model is "O" that identifies Ownership questions.

Ownership questions require a person to take the initiative to answer the knock and open the door to Jesus the Master Coach. It also requires us to take personal responsibility for some key part of our own development or response. When we ask this kind of question, the game of "kick the can down the road" is over. The buck now stops with us and our response will either keep that door closed or open it to new possibilities.

"How might your actions have contributed to this situation."

"Let's say this person never changes. What do you need to do to move on in life even if they don't?"

"What do you think God is forming in your character in this circumstance?"

"Can you think of a positive solution to this problem? What can you do to make that happen?"

"And which of you by being anxious can add a single hour to his span of life?"

Luke 12:25, (ESV)

Ownership questions focus on our taking responsibility for some part of our conversation or some part of our actions. Ownership questions are the keys to these doors:

The Door of personal responsibility versus personal entitlement.

When John was telling me about his stress at work under his new supervisor, I recognized that I was hearing a similar story from others in that department over the last quarter. In that story was the continual use of the word "me" and the absence of the word "we." It seemed as if the resistance to change in that department was rooted in *"What does this mean to me and my comfort zone?"*

I knew these workers were feeling entitled to keeping things as they were, rather than taking responsibility to be part of what they were to become. It was this ownership question, *"What would we want the owner to say about our department six months from now when they celebrate us for helping to lead the company into a successful transition?"* that got the ball rolling in the right direction. "Me" became "we," and "them" became "us."

Personal or professional leadership effectiveness (PLE) begins with taking personal responsibility. It is the foundation to self-governance that minimizes the need for outside micro-management or top-down command and control. Its secret sauce is the willingness to embrace personal constraints so that we can have societal freedoms. It is why the Ten Commandments and Beatitudes are still the keys to freedom and happiness.

In a conversation, relationship, or organizational culture, ownership questions allow us to reset the way we are thinking and behaving to see how our small contribution can become a ripple effect to results and solutions. One small shift away from what I think I deserve or have coming to me can make the difference. It is an ownership question that can start that chain reaction in us and through us.

> One small shift away from what I think I deserve or have coming to me can make the difference. It is an ownership question that can start that chain reaction in us and through us.

In my book, *Confirming the Pastoral Call,* I note the high risks involved in hiring the wrong church staff and the keys to getting it right early and often. One critical ownership question I always ask is, *"Can you describe a disappointment or difficult situation in your vocation in the past and how it shaped who you are or what you do now?"*

What kind of answers am I looking to hear? You guessed it right if you said, *"Anything that reflects ownership or personal responsibility rather than entitlement."* In fact, I could almost predict that a tsunami of pronouns using "I" or "me" instead of "us" or "we" will be an indicator of a mismatch to lead your church.

Every leader has a major story of disappointment or disillusionment. Few leaders have taken the personal responsibility to become better rather than bitter. We need to discover this difference through ownership questions before we hire them.

The Door of collaboration versus competition.

In one of our signature workshops called "I Brand Inside," we discovered that middle and high-school students were willing to be challenged by ownership questions when we showed them stories of people their age collaborating together to make a difference. Twelve videos demonstrated the difference that 14–18-year-olds were making in their local and global worlds. (See example at www.ibrandinside.com)

After each video story, we asked, *"How do their choices show you what difference you can make now when you work with others for a common good?"* Their responses surprised both their peers and their parents and gave our workshop team leaders renewed hope for this theme song that emerged:

> I am not defined by the clothes I wear or the people around me. I am defined by me, by who I am becoming. No one is outside my borders, my circle of honor, my ability to forgive. I am not small enough to create walls. Everyone is my brother or my sister. We are One. I Brand Inside!

The battlegrounds in our campuses and communities have more to do with identity issues than we realize. In fact, we live in a time of one of the greatest identity hacks and theft ever. Identity in Christ has been replaced by identity in gender, race, economics, denomination, politics—all of which threaten to "balkanize" our lives into tribal boundaries that exclude more than include.

Judith Glasser's book, *Conversational Intelligence*, demonstrates the neuro-physical and chemical changes that happen in the three-foot zone in personal interactions. The power to create collaboration and trust is maximized when we take ownership for our part of the conversational climate in our churches and companies. That is why I train all my staff to answer this ownership question each week and report to staff meetings on the results: *"How can my conversations this week cause others to feel prized and encouraged as important parts of a team?"*

> We live in a time of one of the greatest identity hacks and theft ever. Identity in Christ has been replaced by identity in gender, race, economics, denomination, politics—all of which threaten to "balkanize" our lives into tribal boundaries that exclude more than include.

My high-school wrestling coach brought out the best in me when he would ask me, *"Umidi, what do you need to do today to own that mat for our team?"* That question changed my focus from personal competition to team collaboration. I was still competing but for a different reason. Believe me, it made the difference in the last 30 seconds that seemed like an eternity!

Ownership questions allow us to "own the mat" in our lives. We begin to see how we can move beyond the solo competition model of success to create "collaboration zones" that bring out the best in each other. Jesus the Master Coach opens doors to redefine success from being best "in the world" to being best "for the world."

Where will you "own the mat" this week? How will you transform what will happen in your "three-foot" zone? What ownership questions can you design for your staff or team that will cause them to be the best "for the world"?

CATEGORY FOUR in the D.O.O.R. model is "R" that identifies Revealing questions.

Revealing questions enable us to rethink a situation from a new perspective, a different point of view. They also bring to light what is in our heart and what values we are living out.

"What does your response to this say about who you are or what you are called to do?"

"Can you express what about this situation stops or hinders you?"

"When you kick your feet out of bed in the morning and before they touch the floor, you think about going to work today. What are you really looking forward to?"

Many of us are, or know people who are, not clear on what they really think or believe until they are asked questions that help them process and talk it out. They need to hear themselves in order to really know themselves and then own the consequences of their decisions and choices.

An all-knowing God certainly knew what Adam had done, where he was hiding, and why he was covering his newly discovered shame/nakedness. Instead of commanding him to "come out from behind that bush in the name of Jesus, you sinner" He chose to ask this ownership question:

> And they heard the sound of the Lord God walking in the garden in the cool of the day, and the man and his wife hid themselves from the presence of the Lord God among the trees of the garden. But the Lord God called to the man and said to him, **"Where are you?**
>
> Genesis 3:8-9

The more that Adam, the first verbal processor, talked, the more he started owning his story, even though the pain of that ownership caused him to offload his responsibility to Eve. Often, after we ask an ownership question, we need to be still and let silence do the heavy lifting. It is in that pause, that "Selah," that some of the most powerful work of ownership is accomplished.

I often say this to discerning or prophetic people who do not understand the power of the revealing question; "Just because you see it, doesn't mean you say it."

Often, after we ask an ownership question, we need to be still and let silence do the heavy lifting. It is in that pause, that "Selah," that some of the most powerful work of ownership is accomplished.

You may see where a person has hidden or discerned what they are trying to process, but that does not give you the green light to tell them. A better choice is to follow our Master Coach's approach and ask a revealing question. When they see it, they will own it. When they process it, they will not forget it. When we take our cue from God in the garden and Jesus in the Gospels, we will have a lasting influence everywhere we go.

> A better choice is to follow our Master Coach's approach and ask a revealing question. When they see it, they will own it. When they process it, they will not forget it. When we take our cue from God in the garden and Jesus in the Gospels, we will have a lasting influence everywhere we go.

"Why do you see the speck that is in your brother's eye, but do not notice the log that is in your own eye?"

Matthew 7:3, (ESV)

Seeing other perspectives is one of the greatest results of revealing questions. This is what Jesus was seeking to accomplish in this revealing question that gets to the issue of making judgments on others. We project our limited perspective on others primarily because we lack the revelation in our blind spots that there are other perspectives that can be chosen. A revealing question can snap us out of our "locked and loaded" sight, sometimes in a jolting or disruptive manner.

Take a pen or pencil and hold it at arm's-length while you look at a distant object. That is one perspective. Now pull your arm in until the pencil touches your nose and try looking at the same object. Wow, that perspective makes a huge difference! By magnifying the pencil up close, we can barely see the object we want to see clearly. Many times, a revealing question shows us what we have prematurely or preemptively chosen to magnify. Once we see it, we then can choose to minimize it and viola, we can see another's point of view in an honoring and redemptive way. The end result may be nothing less than a breakthrough, reconciliation, and restoration.

Whether or not I am face to face or on a live call, I have a visual method of making this happen for clients. I often help people choose the perspective or options that were not available to them until they saw them as a result of the revealing question. Here is the visual that I use:

Circle the Compass

"Let's stand up and both of us face north. Describe one perspective or one option you can have in response to this person or situation. What does this option or perspective do for you or them in a positive way? What are any downsides of choosing this perspective or option?

"Now let's face south. What is the opposite or 180-degree different option or perspective you can choose in response? What different upsides or downsides come into play if you choose this option?"

Most people can only come up with two options which put them in a dilemma. They feel like they are between a rock and a hard place, a lose/lose double bind. This is where the revealing question shines. It is here that another set of perspectives can come to light and new possibilities that were not there can be found.

"Okay, let's face east. What is another option or perspective that you can choose? Nothing coming to mind? What if you described an option or perspective that they would choose? If you were paying a consultant to give you creative options, what possible out-of-the-box idea would they offer? If you looked at this from the perspective of ten or twenty years from now, what direction could you choose that you would be proud of later? What direction could you take that you sense would be most pleasing to God?"

At this point, these revealing questions are starting to generate new ideas and thoughts as the person is gazing at that point along the compass. They can describe the upside and downside of that perspective, but this is still not the time to come up with choosing one over the other.

"Let's face west. Is there another option or perspective you can see? Nothing yet? What if you combined any of the options already given in some creative way? Can you describe that combination? What is the upside and downside of that option for you or the situation?"

At this point, we have circled the compass with four options. There still could be more. If the person cannot come up with any new ones, you could ask permission to offer a few without selling them on it. If they agree, then you could try northwest or southeast.

Let's say you have asked revealing questions that have resulted in moving from two perspectives or options to seven. Now is the time to walk with the person, actually or figuratively, to the edge where they can get an up-close look and feel for each of these options. They can "try them on for size" and sense how it feels and fits them.

> "Here we are at the edge of the shore looking southeast. What does it feel like to think or behave in this direction? How does this perspective challenge your comfort zone or excite your sense of adventure? What would your future be like if this perspective became your preferred future?"

After spinning around the dial and going out to the edge on each of these with revealing questions we begin to see why Jesus the Master Coach method is so powerful. For the first time for many, they have a new sense of hope, a new energy of creativity and possibility, and a new freedom of options that have broken their self-limitations. This could be a good time to let them think through what their new narrative in their life could be as a result of choosing wisely.

> "Which one of these options could you choose that would bring out your best and leave behind your mediocre? Having described the positives and negatives for each, which one are you most motivated to go for? How can you gather support, encouragement, and accountability to make today's choice tomorrow's milestone in your life?"

Now we have our own app in Jesus' D.O.O.R. model that gives a new understanding of His call to us:

> ...Behold, I have set before you an **open door**, which no one is able to shut...
>
> Rev. 3:8

Through the 100 questions of Jesus the Master Coach in the gospels we have a new door to enter. This is the doorway to understanding how His master coach strategy changed the conversation, changed the relationship, and changed the culture He was called to influence.

Our ongoing emphasis on only the content from Jesus the Teacher cannot get us to our promised land of influence in our time and on our watch. It is in understanding the context of transformational reflection, dialogue, and perspective shift that Jesus the Master Coach brings to us that has been missing.

Without embracing the methodology found in the questions of Jesus the Master Coach, we have inadvertently shifted the Great Commission into the Great Omission. We majored on the teaching content and minored on the relational questioning context to the point of acquiring knowledge by omitting application. We have been blindsided to omitting this unique pedagogy that helps us observe, obey, put into practice, and integrate the power of questions. The end result is a minimized influence in our families, churches, communities, and culture.

> And Jesus came and said to them, "All authority in heaven and on earth has been given to me. Go therefore and make disciples of all nations, baptizing them in the name of the Father and of the Son and of the Holy Spirit, teaching them **to observe all that I have commanded you**. And behold, I am with you always, to the end of the age."
>
> Matthew 28: 18-20

Let's restore the Great Commission by doing less "teach, teach, teach..." and doing more of "obey, obey, obey..." One missing key is Ask More, Tell Less.

Without embracing the methodology found in the questions of Jesus the Master Coach, we have inadvertently shifted the Great Commission into the Great Omission. We majored on the teaching content and minored on the relational questioning context to the point of acquiring knowledge by omitting application.

NOTE: Readers can refer to Appendix for the 100 Questions of Jesus in the D.O.O.R. Categories

Application Questions

1. How can my conversations this week cause others to feel prized and encouraged as important parts of a team? What change in my role in ownership would make this happen more regularly?

2. Where will you "own the mat" this week? How will you transform what will happen in your "three-foot" zone? What ownership questions can you design for your staff or team that will cause them to be the best "for the world"?

3. What does this statement say to you about the power of revealing questions: *"Just because you see it, doesn't mean you say it."*

4. How has this chapter helped you redefine the most common verses often quoted from our pulpits in Matthew 28:18?

For FREE additional materials on the topics of
this book please go to this link:

https://lifeforming.net/jmcresources

Chapter 6

Jesus' Questions
Revive our Heart

ANY BIBLE STUDENT WITH A PULSE has contemplated the magnitude of the biblical values and theology addressed in this chapter. Few have connected the dots to how they are transmitted through questions and conversations. We have categorized the questions of Jesus in the resource section and will give you the meaning of these biblical value categories in this chapter.

The following is not for those with a Ph.D. in Theology but for the serious man or woman who must make a daily difference in our polarized generation. While our fake social media is reaping an addicted ADD culture, we can be "good news" with the values that we bring to any interaction. Armed with a biblical understanding of what is behind the questions of Jesus, we will not be disarmed by the small thinking that this must be some western business world coaching technique applied to the church.

Coaching was birthed for the church and through the church to communicate the aliveness of the Word of God in any context, with or without using chapter and verse.

> You are our epistle written in our hearts, known and **read by** all men.
>
> 2 Corinthians 3:2

Coaching was birthed for the church and through the church to communicate the aliveness of the Word of God in any context, with or without using chapter and verse.

Jesus the Master Coach lives today and is bearing fruit through us that will remain. The following biblical values are being seen, heard, and read daily by everyone who comes within our three to ten-foot zone. By powering our interactions and conversations with questions that communicate these values, our words will not fall to the ground. Instead, they will accelerate our influence at home and at work.

Incarnation Questions: "Being Fully Present"

Alan is a seasoned high-school music educator in one of our roughest school districts with unmotivated and troubled youth. The last few years have taken a toll on him, including hospital stays for stress and high blood pressure. He knew he could not last much longer to reach retirement time and was seeking to switch school systems in a last attempt to find a better student population who would appreciate where he was coming from and where he could take them musically.

And then he realized the power of Jesus questions powered by the biblical value of the incarnation. Here is how he put it:

> "For years I was frustrated that my students did not appreciate my perspective of music mastery. Few were connecting to my agenda of expertise and performance. They did not resonate with my world of choir performances that were judged on music mastery. Even the gifted ones did not have the passion to perform and were not "all-in" to my frame of reference from my former career of professional productions. I spent too much energy and fret over trying to get them to where I was instead of being fully present to where they were."

When Alan shifted his questions from teaching students to enter his world to understanding and communicating in the context of their world the scales fell off his eyes and his stressed and hardened heart began to soften and enlarge for them.

> "I realized that my new goal was not music mastery but growth and development of the person and their potential. I came down to where they were and left my world to fully enter their world. Something had to shift in me first before they were able to shift gears and accelerate in their performance in my class."

For the first time in a decade, his class failed only a few students out of the 108 in his three sections. He had more "A" and "B" students than ever. The students were eager and recovered their passion for life and learning. Alan is healthy and making a living doing what he loves. His colleagues are seeking him out to know the difference. He knows it is in understanding and applying the methods of Jesus the Master Coach.

What every Ambassador for Christ must be and do with intention and focus is to be 100% "fully present" in our conversations. Rather than live in our own worlds, we must enter the world of those we are serving.

> He had equal status with God but didn't think so much of himself that he had to cling to the advantages of that status no matter what. Not at all. When the time came, he set aside the privileges of deity and took on the status of a slave, became human! Having become human, he stayed human. It was an incredibly humbling process. He didn't claim special privileges. Instead, he lived a selfless, obedient life and then died a selfless, obedient death— and the worst kind of death at that: a crucifixion.
>
> Philippians 2:6-8, (The Message)

Through the use of "Incarnational Questions" Jesus was able to leave His frame of reference, His privileged status, His point of view from the throne. He daily fully entered into the worldview, mindset, and heart attitude of anyone in His conversational zone. His questions kept Him focused on who was in front of Him and the kingdom opportunity that had to be seized in that exchange.

Why not let Him show you the courage to be "all in" in the next conversational opportunity you have with a family member or co-worker. It does not have to be long to be effective. Our Emmaus road, Samaritan road, and Damascus road opportunities each day just take the courage to show up. Because Alan fully showed up to his students, they eagerly grew up into their best selves in spite of their worst circumstances.

Our Emmaus road, Samaritan road, and Damascus road opportunities each day just take the courage to show up.

Transformation Questions: "Renewing Worldviews"

> Don't become so well-adjusted to your culture that you fit into it without even thinking. Instead, fix your attention on God. You'll be changed from the inside out. Readily recognize what he wants from you, and quickly respond to it. Unlike the culture around you, always dragging you down to its level of immaturity, God brings the best out of you, develops well-formed maturity in you.
>
> Romans 12:2 (The Message)

The Emmaus road disciples had a "worldview" conflict. They put all their hope in an earthly kingdom with Jesus the Revolutionary overthrowing Rome and putting them in charge. When Jesus asked them in Luke 24:15-17, *"What kind of conversations are you having…"* he was appearing as Jesus the Master Coach who challenged that worldview. Their transformation began by renewing their thinking about their definitions of the kingdom.

The foundation of transformational questions is defining what we mean by the words we use. Everything revolves around meanings of words and the way those words and feelings are communicated.

> The foundation of transformational questions is defining what we mean by the words we use.

Anita thought she understood what success meant and it was not getting a "B" in her classes. After all, she was brought up at every dinner meal with her father asking each of her siblings, "So what did you do today?" Her understanding of that question was, "So what did you accomplish today?" and by the time it always got around to her it seemed like everyone else had done so much more. She entered the university with a definition of success as how much you do in comparison to others.

On the first day of her class with me she was challenged to redefine success when I said; *"Here is how you get an A in my class. Do this, and you get it because I do not compare you with others. What I want you to decide is the answer to this question, **"What does getting an "A" mean to you and what does not getting an "A" mean to you?"** If it means ruining your health, neglecting your* *relationships, and stunting your spiritual growth, then some of you should choose to get a "B." That would be a success for you and for me."*

That day was the beginning of a mind renewal for Anita that enabled her to redefine success as "growth and change in the Kingdom of God" rather than "accomplishing more than her peers." It all began with a Jesus the Master Coach approach with a transformational question.

There is an Anita waiting for you today to ask a transformational question that will become a milestone marker in the way they are thinking. What if you jotted that question down right now and trusted the Holy Spirit for the right time and place to ask it?

Edification Questions: "Building up what has been torn down"

> Therefore, let us pursue the things which make for peace and the
> things by which one may edify another.
>
> Romans 14:19

Slavery had torn down the fabric of democracy in England until Wilberforce worked his whole life to eradicate it in England. He saw Parliament abolish it only a few weeks before his death.

In America, slavery was tearing down the fabric of our democracy and was the leading issue that brought the greatest national disaster in our history, the Civil War. The church had lost its prophetic voice and mission and failed to mend and build up the nation to bring healing to the land. Except for the Quakers.

This first denomination to abolish slavery came as a result of a Jesus the Master Coach approach. At every annual meeting, delegates stood up to ask powerful edification questions. Here is one of them:

"What does the institution of slavery bind up to our children's children?"

By raising questions that enabled a picture of a preferred future for coming generations, this small group of early Jesus followers built up the body of Christ in their day to be bold and courageous. This edification question built up the biblical value that had long been torn down.

> Then God said, "Let us make man in **our image**, according to our
> likeness;"
>
> Genesis 1:26

What does it mean in our daily lives to build up what has been torn down? From a creation foundation, it means to take from Jesus the Master Coach the ability to celebrate God's image in others, even when that image has been torn down by the devil, the culture, or even our own low self-esteem.

> But he, wanting to justify himself, said to Jesus, "And who is my neighbor?
>
> Luke 10:29

> So, which of these three do you think was neighbor to him who fell among the thieves?
>
> Luke 10:36

The Samaritans and the Jews did not build each other up and frankly, did not believe it was possible in their day. Jesus turned the whole cultural conversation on its head with this parable and this key edification question in verse 36. It built up a picture of a reconciliation that has application in our day and age of globally torn ethnic and cultural relationships.

Some of my colleagues in senior positions of leadership have a hard time with edification because they believe people have to earn it to deserve it. They only build up those who have proven worthy of such esteem. Here is the answer to that posture from the Master Coach Himself:

> You know that the rulers of the Gentiles lord it over them, and those who are great exercise authority over them. Yet it shall not be so among you; but whoever desires to become great among you, let him be your servant. And whoever desires to be first among you, let him be your slave— just as the Son of Man did not come to be served, but to serve, and to give His life a ransom for many.
>
> Matthew 20:25-28

Servant-hearted leadership builds people up, and the role of questions is a primary way to do it. I have been accused at times of "flattery" because I ask questions from an edification perspective. My critics have no idea of how long I was addicted to a well-developed sarcasm with people that humorously tore down and left no one built up. It took the biblical value and the heart of God to deliver me from this. Edification is the antidote in my life for keeping me on the side of biblical wholeness.

Edification is the antidote in my life for keeping me on the side of biblical wholeness.

Equipping Questions: "Realigning & Reframing our Perspective"

> And He Himself gave some to be apostles, some prophets, some evangelists, and some pastors and teachers, for the equipping of the saints for the work of ministry, for the edifying of the body of Christ.
>
> Ephesians 4:11-12

Associating with successful people is a key way to expand your own horizons on what is possible in your own life. I have had the privilege of interacting with men and women who have the combination of humility and "can do" faith, even in the waning years of their careers. Like Caleb, at 85, whose biblical declaration "Give me my mountain," I want to hang around leaders who are finishing well. Research reinforces that if you have your health, then the most productive years of your life are 65-75 and the second is 75-85.

> And now, behold, the Lord has kept me alive, as He said, these forty-five years, ever since the Lord spoke this word to Moses while Israel wandered in the wilderness; and now, here I am this day, eighty-five years old. As yet I am as strong this day as on the day that Moses sent me; just as my strength was then, so now is my strength for war, both for going out and for coming in. Now therefore, give me this mountain of which the Lord spoke in that day; for you heard in that day how the Anakim were there, and that the cities were great and fortified. It may be that the Lord will be with me, and I shall be able to drive them out as the Lord said.
>
> Joshua 14:10-12

Those leaders who have used equipping questions have helped me understand that my perspective of their success needed to be adjusted. They were not overnight wonders or instant heroes. Instead, the whole story of their lives and career revealed the price they have paid to have the influence opportunity set before them. They equipped me by aligning my admiration with a sobering sense of whether I am prepared to pay the price they did. Caleb tasted the promised land as a spy but then, had to wait outside of it for 40 years because of the unbelief and complaining of God's people generated by his SEAL team comrades report to them.

> But the men who had gone up with him said, "We are not able to go up against the people, for they are stronger than we." And they gave the children of Israel a bad report of the land which they had spied out, saying, "The land through which we have gone as spies is a land that devours its inhabitants, and all the people whom we saw in it are men of great stature. There we saw the giants (the descendants of Anak came from the giants); and we were like grasshoppers in our own sight, and so we were in their sight." So all the congregation lifted up their voices and cried, and the people wept that night. And all the children of Israel complained against Moses and Aaron, and the whole congregation said to them, "If only we had died in the land of Egypt! Or if only we had died in this wilderness! Why has the Lord brought us to this land to fall by the sword, that our wives and children should become victims? Would it not be better for us to return to Egypt?" So they said to one another, "Let us select a leader and return to Egypt."
>
> Numbers 13:31-14:1

Jesus equipped His disciples, then the Holy Spirit who He sent to us, equips us to face the giants in our lives as we seek to influence and impact the mountains of our time. His equipping questions are like going to the chiropractor to adjust our spine, whether we think we need to or not. Once we are adjusted, we have a posture that is alert and prepared for the unknown... like the time I left my chiropractor's office and was rear-ended by someone texting at 40 miles per hour. If I had not been so well adjusted, I would have been taken out.

> And He said to her, "What do you wish?"
> She said to Him, "Grant that these two sons of mine may sit, one on Your right hand and the other on the left, in Your kingdom."

But Jesus answered and said, "You do not know what you ask. **Are you able to drink the cup that I am about to drink, and be baptized with the baptism that I am baptized with?"**

Matt 20:21-22

I want to fully equip others by the kind of Jesus the Master Coach questions that give them the whole picture of success and not just the celebration sound-bite picture. We need these questions that will prepare us for the things that we did not see coming so that we are not taken out prematurely in our assignments.

Jesus drank the cup of unjust criticism that would cause many in our time with an "entitlement mentality" to complain and protest rather than take up our cross. By putting those questions to those we love and serve, we equip them for facing the giants by those who would unjustly ruin their reputation. These questions will enable us to be standing when the dust settles, fully aligned and equipped for the most productive years of our lives.

> We need these questions that will prepare us for the things that we did not see coming so that we are not taken out prematurely in our assignments.

Application Questions

1. How does Alan's story of being fully present help you in the way you can ask those you are teaching, training, or serving?

2. As we deal with fake news and conflicting worldviews in our conversations, how could taking the time to define what we mean by the words we are using help us to converse more effectively?

3. When you are "edified," what feelings would describe that experience? How could you target your questions and conversations to bring that experience to others? Is there any mindset that you have had with edification that this chapter has helped to adjust?

4. With one definition of "equipping" being to align or adjust, how might your questions adjust another's definition of success or happiness this week?

For FREE additional materials on the topics of
this book please go to this link:

https://lifeforming.net/jmcresources

Chapter 7
Jesus' Questions
Revive our Heart (Part 2)

Identity Formation Questions: "Celebrating Uniqueness"

> Oh yes, you shaped me first inside, then out;
> you formed me in my mother's womb.
> I thank you, High God—you're breathtaking!
> Body and soul, I am marvelously made!
> I worship in adoration—what a creation!
> You know me inside and out,
> you know every bone in my body;
> You know exactly how I was made, bit by bit,
> how I was sculpted from nothing into something."
>
> Psalms 139:13-15, (The Message)

Most new member classes in our churches give people a simple spiritual gift test. The seven motivations in Romans 12, Teacher, Perceiver, Giver, Server, Exhorter, Administrator, and Compassion are a reflection of the multi-faceted reflection of the full character of God that He expresses in His church. We need all of these expressed to get all of God expressed through us. Churches basically intend to help people find their most productive place of service by areas of ministry that best fits their unique design from birth. Gift identification is a good start, but gift implementation is the missing piece.

Naming our gift from an assessment results in that tool collecting dust on a bookshelf in the church office or our files. What is needed is further training to help couples, families, teams, church plants, and staff know and appreciate all the variety of combinations of how God has formed us. That results in learning and celebrating other's gift mixes rather than simply tolerating them. We do this in a signature course called "behavioral intelligence."

Emily and Jeff were so excited in our first pre-marital class as they described how each other's perspectives and gifting so completed their own. They felt like they were a match made in heaven as they talked about how ideal their points of view and conversations made them feel. One year after their marriage, they were trying to understand why the *ideal* had become an *ordeal*. It seemed like they were conflicted in their decisions, spending their emotions trying to get the other person to come over to the other's point of view. What attracted them in the beginning had now become a key source of friction and stress. Maximum celebration had shifted to minimum toleration.

When Emily was given some interactive training on how to see life from Jeff's gift mix, and when Jeff did the same with Emily's, something happened in their spirit and hearts. They no longer just tolerated the tension that different gift mixes produced, but they celebrated the completeness of facing life with both gift mixes in full operation. Now they discovered how to mutually submit to one another, and how to have a ministry "as a couple" that impacted others beyond their hopes and dreams!

> Turning his head, Peter noticed the disciple Jesus loved following right behind. When Peter noticed him, he asked Jesus, "Master, what's going to happen to him?"
>
> Jesus said, **"If I want him to live until I come again, what's that to you? You—follow me."**
>
> John 21:20-22

The Master Coach does not have a "one-size fits all" approach to His disciples but a "tailor-made" plan of working with each of our creation designed gift-mixes that is unique to our formation.

The Master Coach does not have a "one-size fits all" approach to His disciples but a "tailor-made" plan of working with each of our creation designed gift-mixes that is unique to our formation.

Some research has determined that most of what we do can be done by others, especially those trained to do what we can do. However, there is a unique 10-15% contribution that only we can make based on our unique Psalm 139 design. When we add who we are designed to be with who the Holy Spirit anoints us to be, that is a major unique anointing that no one else can duplicate. Like Eric Liddell, the famous Olympic runner depicted in the in *Chariots of Fire* declared, "God made me fast. And when I run, I feel God's pleasure!"

Identity Questions: Identity-In-Christ before any other Identity

> In Christ's family there can be no division into Jew and non-Jew, slave and free, male and female. Among us you are all equal. That is, we are all in a common relationship with Jesus Christ.
>
> Galatians 3:28, (The Message)

Let's Celebrate the "one of a kind" creation in us and in those we serve. Jesus the Master coach shows us the way and will make a way for others who feel like a number rather than a name. After all, He alone does the most unique thing imaginable among all the world religions when He says:

> He calls his own sheep **by name** and leads them out. When he gets them all out, he leads them and they follow because they are familiar with his voice. They won't follow a stranger's voice but will scatter because they aren't used to the sound of it.
>
> John 10:3-5

Following our Master means we can ask these kinds of identity questions every day:

"What is your name?"

"What is the meaning of your name, if you know it?"

"Why did your parents give you that name, if you know?"

"What name or nickname would you like to be known for, if not your given name?"

Roland was being shaped by his peers to conform to the identity politics of the secular campus culture where he began the process of magnifying race, gender, and political party over who he was in Christ. There were plenty of campus unrest stories across the nation to support his newly found sense of "cause" ...until he met Bruce.

Bruce was one of our campus ministry staff who knew who he was in Christ. He was able to catalyze authenticity in Bruce by sharing his own journey of being bullied by identity politics and to find his highest cause in the freedom in Christ to bring true and lasting justice. It all came together when Bruce borrowed from the Master Coach playbook with this key question:

> What good would it do to get everything you want and lose you,
> the real you?
>
> Mark 8:36, (The Message)

Roland began the journey of redefining himself that day. He became a leader that was secure in Christ and would not take offense or take on another's offense. His energy for justice came out of a new centering and alignment of his identity-in-Christ, and he led many to do so without bitterness, anger, or entitlement. He had discovered that he was only one conversation away from a breakthrough into His true identity.

Roland's story inspired me to develop one of our signature transformational trainings for middle- and high-school youth called *I BRAND INSIDE* described on page 38. We show 12 short videos of 12-18 aged students who are changing their worlds through causes they have started or helped advance. We help them see how all of this and more comes out of a true identity in Christ Jesus.

Dreams and Vision Questions: Opening the eyes of our heart

> Now is my soul troubled. And what shall I say? 'Father, save me
> from this hour? But for this **purpose** I have come to this hour.
>
> John 12:27

Jesus was clear about His purpose, and He was not hesitant to talk about it. One of the most effective ways to follow Jesus the Master Coach is to probe people with the questions that get to the "Why" behind the "What."

The G.R.O.W. model, introduced in the iconic book, *Performance Coaching*, is the 101 level for training coaches to help clients achieve their "What." It immediately takes fuzzy aspirations and enables clients to sharpen their performances. It begins with **Goals**, moves to examining the **Reality** of the context for these goals, explores **Options** to go after these goals, and determines the **Will** or willingness level to actually begin and stay the course to goal achievement. It can be done in a five-minute or 55-minute conversation and even works well with teenagers. One of the reasons for its long shelf life is that it forces us to make our goals S.M.A.R.T.—specific, measurable, achievable, relevant, and time-specific.

But what if my goal ladders are leaning against the wrong walls? What if we rushed to "get-er-done" and did not step back and ask the purpose questions ahead of time? You guessed it... wasted time, energy, money, and focus. Simply because we got ahead of our Master Coach approach.

The "Dreamfire Experience" was my answer to this challenge. Designed to help people discover the key intersection of their purpose and passion, it gives a series of reflective questions that enabled groups or individuals to clearly define their "Why" before setting goals for their "What."

Gene just stepped down from his high-school coaching position when he called me about his goals in life. It did not take me long to realize that he had never given himself the time and space to get clarity on his purpose and passion, even though he was in his mid-50s. Four weeks later, he was like a teenager getting his driver's license.

> "I just realized that my dream is to help people recreate their lost aspirations. I am going to give myself to learning how to ask more *Why* questions than *What* questions!"

Gene just finished our premiere coach certification course called ACT that is ICF approved. Over 10,000 in 30 countries and 15 languages are shouting out with him as they have done the same over the last 22 years.

One of my students put it so succinctly when she summarized this dynamic Master Coach approach with this statement:

> "If your Why does not make you Cry, the price of commitment is always too high."

Knowing our purpose, and the passion for making it come to pass will enable us to pay whatever price is necessary to achieve the goals to get there.

Knowing our purpose, and the passion for making it come to pass will enable us to pay whatever price is necessary to achieve the goals to get there.

Honor Questions: The lost key of favor with God and men

> **Honor your father** and your mother, as the Lord your God commanded you, that your days may be long, and that it may go well with you in the land that the Lord your God is giving you.
>
> Deuteronomy 5:16

> And when his parents saw him, they were astonished. And his mother said to him, "Son, why have you treated us so? Behold, your father and I have been searching for you in great distress." And he said to them, "Why were you looking for me? Did you not know that ᵉI must be in my Father's house?" And they did not understand the saying that he spoke to them. And he went down with them and came to Nazareth and was submissive to them. And his mother treasured up all these things in her heart.
>
> Luke 2:48-51, (ESV)

I never tire of telling my story of interacting with an ambassador from Israel in my book *Transformational Intelligence: Creating Cultures of Honor at Home and Work*. Here is an excerpt from it:

More recently, I had the privilege of meeting an ambassador from Israel at a public lecture attended by VIPs from various backgrounds. I was there to escort my wife who sang and to carry her heavy keyboard. Because I was her transportation I was invited back to the VIP after the event that was attended by invitation only. Somehow the ambassador singled me out and engaged me in an eight-minute conversation that was extraordinary. Though we were not totally in agreement on his points, it was a powerful conversation that I remember to this day. It seemed as if I was the honored guest and my perspective was sought after and taken as seriously as if I were his boss, the Prime Minister.

I asked my wife on the way home, "What school does an ambassador go to? I think I need to go there and get what he has."

Four years later, my wife was asked to sing again at an event in the capital of our nation that was the goodbye celebration for this gentleman as he was to return home to a new government post. This time I was to both wear a tuxedo and carry the keyboard. I tried to find a way to be excused because I did not want to attend a politically charged meeting, attended by the former Republican leader of the House of Representatives and the present Democratic leader in charge; along with the five hundred guests from all the religious, cultural, and political differences you could gather in one room. I was prepared for the political spin, hype, and posturing that could make for a long evening in a less than comfortable attire.

Sometime during the event, I realized that this was not at all what I expected. The atmosphere was drenched with humility, honor, celebration, and even a sense of family unity around this couple's four-year tenure representing his country to us. As I conversed with the guests at our table, I discovered the key reason. Each of the guests at my table had an extraordinary conversation with the ambassador that had impacted them, similar to what I had experienced, even if it was only a brief exchange.

The final confirmation came when I heard the stories from the platform personalities that basically repeated my experience to the letter. Over five hundred people from every walk of life had been transformed by a conversation with the ambassador. Now they were able to shift the culture of the most politically polarizing part of our country in a meeting, and in their lives, because someone had given them the gift of honor in a relational exchange that was transformational.

After all, over 500 people in that hotel room, like me, were impacted by the ambassador in less than ten minutes.

It takes courage to honor, to be fully present for people. My wife has modeled that to me all of our married life and reminds me when I need a refill in my courage tank. Sometimes, when I am on my laptop, watching a sports game on TV, and talking with her at the same time, she gets up, gently closes my computer, and then looks me right in the eyes as she blocks my view. For the little time we have together each week, she wants me to honor her, to be fully present with her; she is not afraid to fight for the best marriage conversations she can get.

Susan Scott's outstanding book, *Fierce Conversations: Achieving Success at Work & in Life, One Conversation at a Time,* was my wake-up call to my becoming more fully present to honor others. One of the points she makes on being fully present is this story:

> Among the tribes of northern Natal in South Africa, the most common greeting, equivalent to "hello" in English, is the expression: *"sawu bona."* It literally means, "I see you." If you are a member of the tribe, you might reply by saying *"sikhona"* or "I am here." The order of the exchange is important: until you see me, I do not exist. It's as if, when you see me, you bring me into existence.

Now that is a great expression of honor!

Jesus the Master Coach honored us by coming to us. He was and is fully present to us and through us when we ask sincerely, courageously, and curiously with our whole hearts to honor others.

Application Questions

1. How does Emily and Jeff's marital story relate to your own heart ability for celebrating rather than tolerating uniqueness in others?

2. How has your identity been expressed by these questions:
    "What is your name?"
    "What is the meaning of your name if you know it?"
    "Why did your parents give you that name if you know?"
    "What name or nickname would you like to be known for if not your given name?"

3. What dreams or vision questions could you ask that would help someone get to the "why" behind their "what"?

4. What did the story of honoring the Israeli ambassador do to help you with questions and conversations that could make your impact and influence move to that level?

For FREE additional materials on the topics of
this book please go to this link:

https://lifeforming.net/jmcresources

Chapter 8
Jesus' Questions Accelerate Transformational Influence

AT 12 YEARS OLD, Jesus the Master Coach was having an ambassador-level transformational influence. How did He do it? He did it the same way we are to do it today, through asking and questioning. Here is the scene:

> [41] His parents went to Jerusalem every year at the Feast of the Passover. [42] And when He was twelve years old, they went up to Jerusalem according to the custom of the feast. [43] When they had finished the days, as they returned, the Boy Jesus lingered behind in Jerusalem. And Joseph and His mother did not know *it;* [44] but supposing Him to have been in the company, they went a day's journey, and sought Him among *their* relatives and acquaintances. [45] So when they did not find Him, they returned to Jerusalem, seeking Him. [46] Now so it was *that* after three days they found Him in the temple, sitting in the midst of the teachers, **both listening to them and asking them questions**. [47] And all who heard Him were astonished at His understanding and answers. [48] So when they saw Him, they were amazed; and His mother said to Him, "Son, why have You done this to us? Look, Your father and I have sought You anxiously."
>
> [49] And He said to them, "Why did you seek Me? Did you not know that I must **be about My Father's business**?" [50] But they did not understand the statement which He spoke to them.
>
> [51] Then He went down with them and came to Nazareth, and was subject to them, but His mother kept all these things in her

heart. [52] And Jesus increased in wisdom and stature, and in favor with God and men.

Luke 2:41-52

The "business of the Father" for Jesus the Master Coach at 12 was **both listening to them and asking them questions.** At 12, Jesus the Master Coach was doing what he continued to do at 33. He models for us what we can and must do from 12 years on. We are to function as ambassadors who influence by the power of listening and asking. This was the father's business then and it is the father's business now.

Verse 46 says nothing about Jesus instructing them. He was simply "listening and asking questions." Yet they were "amazed at His understanding and His answers."

> # The "business of the Father" for Jesus the Master Coach at 12 was <u>both listening to them and asking them questions</u>. At 12, Jesus the Master Coach was doing what he continued to do at 33. He models for us what we can and must do from 12 years on.

I have confidence that most of the coaches we have trained have been in conversations where they were just "listening and asking them questions" and afterward, the person would say how wise they are, or what great advice they gave them. I know it's happened to me on hundreds of occasions.

Is it possible that Jesus helped the teachers in the temple to arrive at their own conclusions and to gain "understanding" because of the powerful questions He was asking them? In which case, they had no category to place this kind of teaching. Their presupposition was, that in order to learn, you must be instructed by someone greater than yourself in the subject. In this case, the least (a 12-year-old boy) became the greatest, because he became a servant-conversationalist with them all.

Here is a statement that should rock our Sunday School worlds; a key to *"Jesus increasing in wisdom and stature, and in favor with God and men"* is to increase our listening and asking. The unfortunate lack of this focus in our discipleship models has resulted in a void of ambassador-level influence in our culture.

> A key to "Jesus increasing in wisdom and stature, and in favor with God and men" is to increase our listening and asking. The unfortunate lack of this focus in our discipleship models has resulted in a void of ambassador-level influence in our culture.

Questions, and our ability to listen well to the answer, have been compartmentalized to the realm of pastoral care and counseling. We have now defined great leaders as great speakers, vision casters, and CEOs. Jesus defines great leaders as great servants. One of the most powerful ways to serve another is to ask and listen, rather than tell and give advice. The greatest leaders I have experienced have been the greatest listeners. Here is how Jesus puts it:

> And when the ten heard *it,* they began to be greatly displeased with James and John. But Jesus called them to *Himself* and said to them, "You know that those who are considered rulers over the Gentiles lord it over them, and their great ones exercise authority over them. Yet it shall not be so among you; but whoever desires to become great among you shall be your servant.
>
> Mark 10:41-44

At 12 years old, Jesus the Master Coach was doing the father's business of listening and asking at an ambassador level. Most of us need to take a hard look at the foundations of our faith formation and see where our teachers and trainers have missed this key element. The missing foundations will not enable us to have an Ambassador-level influence. Instead, we will dumb down our identity and calling to the irreducible minimum and battle most of our lives with doubts about whether we are making a difference. We will be bullied into a "grasshopper" mentality in our view of the giants we face in our culture today.

> There we saw the giants (the descendants of Anak came from the giants); and we were like **grasshoppers** in our own sight, and so we were in their sight.
>
> Numbers 13:33

> If the **foundations are** destroyed, what can the righteous do?
>
> Psalms 11:3

When we rediscover the Jesus we were never taught, the Jesus we never knew, the Jesus as Master Coach we never saw before, then we can become the Jesus ambassadors to our day that we never thought possible. What would that look like?

> When we rediscover the Jesus we were never taught, the Jesus we never knew, the Jesus as Master Coach we never saw before, then we can become the Jesus ambassadors to our day that we never thought possible.

Ambassadors in the Home

Mark and Ellen knew they had to change the mealtime dynamics in their home. The TV, cell phones, and daily stress of school and work were causing the meal times to be hurried pauses that did not relationally, emotionally, or spiritually refresh. It all changed when they attended a "Real Talk Café" (Conversational Champions)workshop on how to have extraordinary conversations at home and work. They knew the first place they had to change was dinner time. Here is how they put it:

> We made a game out of seeing how well each of our four kids and us as parents could ask more and better questions and listen well to the answers. We started with questions that we put on cards and then had all of us draw from a card deck during our mealtime. Then we had the kids create their own question cards and we all drew from their deck. We did this on the three nights per week we were all home at the dinner table.

Something began to shift around the third week when our kids started asking their friends the question cards they brought with them on the school bus. Then we started asking our kids each night this question, "What question did you ask at school today that your teacher said something like, 'That was a great question'? What did you learn about them from the way they answered?"

All of us, including parents, knew that at any meal time together we would need to be ready to give an answer to, "What great question did you ask today that helped you to learn something new about a person or a subject?"

We started doing a weekly theme, like Star Wars, Ocean animals, where we all came to the dinner table with questions around the theme and an object, or even a dress-up, that emphasized that theme. What was really powerful was to see what happened with our kids' friends whenever they were over in one of those mealtimes. It was like another planet compared to the typical mealtime in their own homes.

Mark and Ellen's kids are now off to college, but the stories of their kids' ambassador-level impact are still being told. From the comments from peers, parents, and teachers in their junior- and high-school years to the feedback from peers, professors, and employers in this present stage of their development, one thing is clear; they have raised up kids that have a unique influence on others. Like Jesus the Master Coach in the temple who was "both listening to them and asking them questions," their kids have "increased in wisdom, stature, and favor with God and men."

Ambassadors in the Church

Harry was a VP in a major corporation in town and was known for his intimidating size and countenance. He had a reputation in college football as an offensive lineman for putting fear in the opposition just by his presence. I will never forget how I felt the first time I met him as an elder of the two-year-old church. He had the people skills of a grizzly bear but the heart of a teddy bear!

The first six months of my new role was when the rubber met the road with my theory of the power of asking and listening like Jesus. If I could help Harry, then this stuff could work for anyone. When I started my first session, I must have shocked him when I said, *"The number one killer of authentic relationships is giving advice that no one is asking for. By asking more and telling less we are honoring others like Jesus did and endearing them to us. Asking questions is the key to enlarging our heart for others."*

I will never forget seeing Harry tear up. At that moment, I knew that he would become my poster child for having an ambassador influence through ambassador-quality questions. Harry became my key ambassador to visitors, new members, and new leaders. Because he embraced the heart and methods of Jesus the Master Coach, his huge heart for others could now overcome his huge intimidating presence.

When Harry prepared and prayed over his questions, he was then able to ask others from a heart of honor and inclusion, even first-timers. He disarmed people's defenses quickly and was my main go-to person for drawing people into our fledgling fellowship. Through Harry's influence and role model to other leaders we grew from 125 to 275 members in less than two years and turned a wounded church into a winning church. Harry was my ambassador of authentic connection!

Ambassadors in the Workplace

Over the last fifty years, we have seen the emergence of great initiatives that are targeting the workplace as the primary litmus test of our ambassador influence. Ministries like "Faith at Work," "Business as Mission," "7 Mountains," "Marketplace Ministry" and others are redefining success for maturing disciples by the difference they are making on their jobs or through their enterprises, rather than simply their home and church.

Though pastors have been slow to embrace any other focus than their battle to maintain and grow vibrant churches in our dysfunctional culture climate, they are beginning to awaken to the need to train their members to influence the secular workplace without using chapter and verse bible references in their language. When we train pastors and church leaders in this new *Real Talk* perspective, we start with teaching them a second language; the language of influencing effectively in "Babylon" rather than just comfortably camping out in "Zion."

> By the rivers of Babylon we sat and wept
> when we remembered Zion'

There on the poplars
we hung our harps
for there our captors asked us for songs,
our tormentors demanded songs of joy;
they said, "Sing us one of the songs of Zion."
How can we sing the songs of the Lord
while in a foreign land?

Psalms 137:1-4, (NIV)

When Mary rediscovered her childlike curiosity through the role of powerful questions, she was able to approach her co-workers without feeling the need to measure her success by quoting the Bible to them. In just a few months her department sensed that she took them and their lives more seriously and felt a new level of care and concern for them. Mary was amazed by the difference when they began to approach her and ask her for her perspective on their life issues. She was even more overwhelmed when she found increased "favor with God and men" by the award she received from her staff at the annual Christmas party. By speaking their language rather than expecting them to speak hers, Mary embraced her calling as an ambassador to the workplace.

> When we train pastors and church leaders in this new *Real Talk* perspective, we start with teaching them a second language; the language of influencing effectively in "Babylon" rather than just comfortably camping out in "Zion."

Ambassadors in the Community

I was so looking forward to preaching in this prominent church in Cape Town until it all fell apart the day I landed in South Africa. Riots broke out across the country as the pride of the "Rainbow Nation" found that South Africans were now destroying the businesses and homes of the resident Africans from neighboring countries. People were fleeing for their lives.

71

The church had to be the first responder because the government was not prepared nor able to get organized quickly. That meant the church where I was to preach had canceled their Sunday service to set up a tent to hold 200 men and another tent for 400 women and children. That's when I knew what my job description became for that week.

Instead of preaching to 5,000, I trained 125 millennial church members in the **"Conversational Champion"** format to be ready to bring reconciliation in the midst of the tension. We commissioned them as ambassadors of community reconciliation and sent them into the townships with the call to minimize tensions through maximizing transformational conversations. The risks were high but the riots they faced needed a radical kingdom approach. There was no other help on the horizon except for them.

The results were astonishing. Lives were saved, and property was spared. These young men and women became heroes and heroines by being fully present to others and enabling them to experience Jesus the Master Coach in their midst. It was a dramatic lesson that prepared me to face my own opportunity for community reconciliation the following year.

Our oceanside city had experienced its first major unrest when college students flooded our streets and violence and destruction broke out. It became national news and tarnished the hard-earned reputation we had developed of a safe family-friendly resort. Nine months later we faced the same college crowd about to come in a few months. That is when I gathered thirteen churches for a combination of prayer and ambassador-level communication training through our Real Talk Café's strategy.

When the students showed up on our boardwalk, they found over 1,000 church members trained as ambassadors, who were sent out two-by-two to start significant conversations with strangers. Many of these conversations brought tears, high-fives, and hugs. More importantly, none of the violence of the previous year was repeated. Like Jesus in the temple at age 12, we had found wisdom and favor with God and men through listening and asking questions.

Ambassadors to the Nations

Jeff was a young Baptist pastor who admitted to having disdain and hatred in his heart for Muslims. Whenever he saw a woman in a Burka, he would recoil and have to pray that he would not blurt out something he would regret. That all changed after he went through our ACT coach training course. That was the beginning of his Ambassador to the Nations calling.

When Jeff posted a video on YouTube about how a Muslim child broke his heart, it went viral. Now, many Muslims around the world are contacting him to help them get over their own animosity toward Americans and Christians. As amazing as that is, it is only the beginning.

Jeff has befriended Imams, Muslim clerics in his city, state, region, and around the world. Those friendships have led to many cultural experiences with Christians and Muslims that have broken down prejudices. Those that he has trained in our relational connecting Jesus the Master Coach methodology have defused tensions among Muslims, Christians, and Jews during increasing times of ethnic and religious violence.

And then this unpretentious and humble young pastor saw the favor of God on him in an unprecedented way. Jeff has been invited several times to interact with the leading officials in Sudan to help end the wars in their ethnically divided countries. He has been received with honor as well as expectation and he has seen results that even our own state-department-trained personnel have not experienced. There is only one explanation I have for this; Jesus the Master Coach is alive and well today as He was in the days that He asked 100 questions on earth that have been captured in the four Gospels.

This same Jesus that has made ambassadors out of Mark and Ellen, Harry, Mary, South African millennials, and Jeff is able to do more abundantly than we can ask or think anytime or anywhere. What has to change is the Jesus we know and become like. Now is the time for Jesus the Master Coach to be fully revealed in the sons and daughters of the Kingdom of God.

For such a time as this.

This same Jesus that has made ambassadors out of Mark and Ellen, Harry, Mary, South African millennials, and Jeff is able to do more abundantly than we can ask or think anytime or anywhere.

Application Questions

1. How does Mark and Ellen's story as ambassadors to the home impact you? How can Jesus the Master Coach approach help you be an ambassador there?

2. How did Harry's story as an ambassador to the church impact you? How can Jesus the Master Coach approach help you be an ambassador there?

3. How did Mary's story as an ambassador to the workplace impact you? How can Jesus the Master Coach approach help you be an ambassador there?

4. How did my story or Jeff's story as an ambassador to the community or nations impact you? How can Jesus the Master Coach approach help you be an ambassador there?

For FREE additional materials on the topics of
this book please go to this link:

https://lifeforming.net/jmcresources

Appendix A

100 Questions Jesus Asked

1. And if you greet your brethren only, what is unusual about that? Do not the unbelievers do the same? (Matt 5:47)

2. Can any of you by worrying add a single moment to your lifespan? (Matt 6:27)

3. Why are you anxious about clothes? (Matt 6:28)

4. Why do you notice the splinter in your brother's eye yet fail to perceive the wooden beam in your own eye? (Matt 7:3)

5. Do people pick grapes from thornbushes or figs from thistles? (Matt 7:16)

6. Why are you terrified? (Matt 8:26)

7. Why do you harbor evil thoughts? (Matt 9:4)

8. Can the wedding guests mourn so long as the bridegroom is with them? (Matt 9:15)

9. Do you believe I can do this? (Matt 9:28)

10. What did you go out to the desert to see? (Matt 11:8-9)

11. To what shall I compare this generation? (Matt 11:16)

12. Which of you who has a sheep that falls into a pit on the Sabbath will not take hold of it and lift it out? (Matt 12:11-12)

13. How can anyone enter a strong man's house and take hold of his possessions unless he first ties up the strong man? (Matt 12:29)

14. You brood of vipers! How can you say good things when you are evil? (Matt 12:34)

15. Who is my mother? Who are my brothers? (Matt 12:48)

16. Why did you doubt? (Matt 14:31)

17. And why do you break the commandments of God for the sake of your tradition? (Matt 15:3)

18. How many loaves do you have? (Matt 15:34)

19. Do you not yet understand? (Matt 16:8-9)

20. Who do people say the Son of Man is? (Matt 16:13)

21. But who do you say that I am? (Matt 16:15)

22. What profit would there be for one to gain the whole world and forfeit his life and what can one give in exchange for his life? (Matt 16:26)

23. O faithless and perverse generation how long must I endure you? (Matt 17:17)

24. Why do you ask me about what is good? (Matt 19:17)

25. Can you drink the cup that I am going to drink? (Matt 20:22)

26. What do you want me to do for you? (Matt 20:32)

27. Did you never read the scriptures? (Matt 21:42)

28. Why are you testing me? (Matt 22:18)

29. Blind fools, which is greater, the gold or the temple that makes the gold sacred....the gift of the altar that makes the gift sacred? (Matt 23:17-19)

30. How are you to avoid being sentenced to hell? (Matt 23:33)

31. Why do you make trouble for the woman? (Matt 26:10)

32. Could you not watch for me one brief hour? (Matt 26:40)

33. Do you think I cannot call upon my Father and he will not provide me at this moment with more than 12 legions of angels? (Matt 26:53-54)

34. Have you come out as against a robber with swords and clubs to seize me? (Matt 26:55)

35. My God, My God, Why have you forsaken me? (Matt 27:46)

36. Why are you thinking such things in your heart? (Mark 2:8)

37. Is a lamp brought to be put under a basket or under a bed rather than on a lamp stand? (Mark 4:21)

38. Who has touched my clothes? (Mark 5:30)

39. Why this commotion and weeping? (Mark 5:39)

40. Are even you likewise without understanding? (Mark 7:18)

41. Why does this generation seek a sign? (Mark 8:12)

42. Do you not yet understand or comprehend? Are your hearts hardened? Do you have eyes and still not see? Ears and not hear? (Mark 8:17-18)

43. How many wicker baskets full of leftover fragments did you pick up? (Mark 8:19)

44. [To the Blind man] Do you see anything? (Mark 8:23)

45. What were you discussing on the way? (Mark 9:33)

46. Salt is good, but what if salt becomes flat? (Mark 9:50)

47. What did Moses command you? (Mark 10:3)

48. Do you see these great buildings? They will all be thrown down. (Mark 13:2)

49. Simon, are you asleep? (Mark 14:37)

50. Why were you looking for me? (Luke 2:49)

51. What are you thinking in your hearts? (Luke 5:22)

52. Why do you call me 'Lord, Lord' and not do what I command? (Luke 6:46)

53. Where is your faith? (Luke 8:25)

54. What is your name? (Luke 8:30)

55. Who touched me? (Luke 8:45)

56. Will you be exalted to heaven? (Luke 10:15)

57. What is written in the law? How do you read it? (Luke 10:26)

58. Which of these three in your opinion was neighbor to the robber's victim? (Luke 10:36)

59. Did not the maker of the outside also make the inside? (Luke 11:40)

60. Friend, who appointed me as your judge and arbiter? (Luke 12:14)

61. If even the smallest things are beyond your control, why are you anxious about the rest? (Luke 12:26)

62. Why do you not judge for yourself what is right? (Luke 12:57)

63. What king, marching into battle would not first sit down and decide whether with ten thousand troops he can successfully oppose another king marching upon him with twenty thousand troops? (Luke 14:31)

64. If therefore you are not trustworthy with worldly wealth, who will trust you with true wealth? (Luke 16:11)

65. Has none but this foreigner returned to give thanks to God? (Luke 17:17-18)

66. Will not God then secure the rights of his chosen ones who call out to him day and night? (Luke 18:7)

67. But when the Son of Man comes, will he find any faith on earth? (Luke 18:8)

68. For who is greater, the one seated a table or the one who serves? (Luke 22:27)

69. Why are you sleeping? (Luke 22:46)

70. For if these things are done when the wood is green, what will happen when it is dry? (Luke 23:31)

71. What are you discussing as you walk along? (Luke 24:17)

72. Was it not necessary that the Messiah should suffer these things and then enter his glory? (Luke 24:26)

73. Have you anything here to eat? (Luke 24:41)

74. What are you looking for? (John 1:38)

75. How does this concern of your affect me? (John 2:4)

76. You are a teacher in Israel and you do not understand this? (John 3: 10)

77. If I tell you about earthly things and you will not believe, how will you believe when I tell you of heavenly things? (John 3: 12)78.

78. Do you want to be well? (John 5:6)

79. How is it that you seek praise from one another and not seek the praise that comes from God? (John 5:44)

80. If you do not believe Moses' writings how will you believe me? (John 5:47)

81. Where can we buy enough food for them to eat? (John 6:5)

82. Does this (teaching of the Eucharist) shock you? (John 6:61-62)

83. Do you also want to leave me? (John 6:67)

84. Why are you trying to kill me? (John 7:19)

85. Woman where are they, has no one condemned you? (John 8:10)

86. Why do you not understand what I am saying? (John 8:43)

87. Can any of you charge me with sin? (John 8:46)

88. If I am telling you the truth, why do you not believe me? (John 8:46)

89. Are there not twelve hours in a day? (John 11:9)

90. Do you believe this? (John 11:26)

91. Do you realize what I have done for you? (John 13:12)

92. Have I been with you for so long and still you do not know me? (John 14:9)

93. Whom are you looking for? (John 18:4)

94. Shall I not drink the cup the Father gave me? (John 18:11)

95. If I have spoken rightly, why did you strike me? (John 18:23)

96. Do you say [what you say about me] on your own or have others been telling you about me? (John 18:34)

97. Have you come to believe because you have seen me? (John 20:29)

98. Do you love me? (John 21:16-17)

99. What if I want John to remain until I come? (John 21:22)

100. What concern is it of yours? (John 21:23)

Appendix B
D.O.O.R Chart of Questions Jesus Asked

D.O.O.R CHART CATEGORY	Direct	Open	Ownership	Revealing
1. Matt 5:47				x
2. Matt 6:27	x			
3. Matt 6:28	x			x
4. Matt 7:3	x		x	
5. Matt 7:16				x
6. Matt 8:26	x	x		x
7. Matt 9:4	x	x	x	x
8. Matt 9:15				x
9. Matt 9:28	x		x	x
10. Matt 11:8-9		x		x
11. Matt 11:16		x		x
12. Matt 12:11-12		x	x	x
13. Matt 12:29				x
14. Matt 12:34	x	x		x
15. Matt 12:48		x		x
16. Matt 14:31	x	x	x	
17. Matt 15:3	x	x	x	
18. Matt 15:34			x	x
19. Matt 16:8-9	x		x	
20. Matt 16:13		x		x

D.O.O.R CHART CATEGORY (continued)	Direct	Open	Ownership	Revealing
21. Matt 16:15	x	x		x
22. Matt 16:26		x		x
23. Matt 17:17	x		x	
24. Matt 19:17		x		x
25. Matt 20:22	x		x	x
26. Matt 20:32		x	x	
27. Matt 21:42	x		x	
28. Matt 22:18		x	x	
29. Matt 23:17-19				x
30. Matt 23:33	x	x		
31. Matt 26:10		x	x	x
32. Matt 26:40	x		x	
33. Matt 26:53-54	x			x
34. Matt 26:55			x	x
35. Matt 27:46		x		
36. Mark 2:8			x	
37. Mark 4:21				x
38. Mark 5:30			x	
39. Mark 5:39		x		
40. Mark 7:18	x			
41. Mark 8:12		x		
42. Mark 8:17-18	x		x	
43. Mark 8:19	x			
44. Mark 8:23			x	
45. Mark 9:23		x	x	x
46. Mark 9:50				x
47. Mark 10:3		x		x
48. Mark 13:2	x			
49. Mark 14:37			x	
50. Luke 2:49			x	x
51. Luke 5:22-23	x			x
52. Luke 6:46	x		x	
53. Luke 8:25	x		x	

D.O.O.R CHART CATEGORY (continued)	Direct	Open	Ownership	Revealing
54. Luke 8:30	x			x
55. Luke 8:45			x	
56. Luke 10.15	x			x
57. Luke 10:26			x	x
58. Luke 10:36		x		x
59. Luke 11:40	x		x	
60. Luke 12:14	x		x	
61. Luke 12:26		x		x
62. Luke 12:57	x			x
63. Luke 14:31		x		x
64. Luke 16:11	x			x
65. Luke 17:17-18		x	x	
66. Luke 18:7	x			
67. Luke 18:8				x
68. Luke 22:27	x			x
69. Luke 22:46	x		x	
70. Luke 23:31		x		x
71. Luke 24:17	x	x		x
72. Luke 24:26				x
73. Luke 24:41				x
74. John 1:38	x	x		
75. John 2:4	x			x
76. John 3:10	x		x	
77. John 3:12	x			x
78. John 5:6	x		x	
79. John 5:44	x		x	
80. John 5:47	x		x	
81. John 6:5		x		x
82. John 6:61-62	x			x
83. John 6:67	x		x	
84. John 7:19	x		x	
85. John 8:10		x		x
86. John 8:43	x			x

D.O.O.R CHART CATEGORY (continued)	Direct	Open	Ownership	Revealing
87. John 8:46	x			
88. John 8:46	x			
89. John 11:9		x		x
90. John 11:26	x		x	
91. John 13:12		x		x
92. John 14:9	x			x
93. John 18:4	x			x
94. John 18:11		x		x
95. John 18:23	x			x
96. John 18:34	x		x	
97. John 20:29		x		x
98. John 21:16-17		x		x
99. John 21:22	x		x	
100. John 21:23	x		x	

Appendix C

Coaching Values Chart of Questions Jesus Asked

COACHING VALUES CHART CATEGORIES	Value 1 Believe in Others	Value 2 God Initiates Change	Value 3 Individual Responsibility	Value 4 Transformation is Experiential	Value 5 Authentic Relationships	Value 6 Unique Design	Value 7 See Others Like Father Does
1. Matt 5:47	x	x		x	x		
2. Matt 6:27		x	x	x			
3. Matt 6:28				x			x
4. Matt 7:3	x			x	x		x
5. Matt 7:16		x	x	x	x		x
6. Matt 8:26		x	x	x			x
7. Matt 9:4		x	x	x	x		x
8. Matt 9:15			x				
9. Matt 9:28		x	x	x			x
10. Matt 11:8-9			x	x	x		x
11. Matt 11:16		x	x		x		x
12. Matt 12:11-12		x	x			x	x
13. Matt 12:29			x				x
14. Matt 12:34		x	x		x		x
15. Matt 12:48	x		x	x	x	x	x
16. Matt 14:31	x	x		x		x	x
17. Matt 15:3			x	x			x
18. Matt 15:34	x		x	x			
19. Matt 16:8-9			x	x			x
20. Matt 16:13		x	x				x

COACHING VALUES CHART CATEGORIES (continued)	Value 1 Believe in Others	Value 2 God Initiates Change	Value 3 Individual Responsibility	Value 4 Transformation is Experiential	Value 5 Authentic Relationships	Value 6 Unique Design	Value 7 See Others Like Father Does
21. Matt 16:15		x	x	x	x		x
22. Matt 16:26			x		x		x
23. Matt 17:17			x		x		
24. Matt 19:17					x		x
25. Matt 20:22			x	x	x		x
26. Matt 20:32	x	x		x		x	
27. Matt 21:42		x	x				
28. Matt 22:18		x	x	x			
29. Matt 23:17-19				x			x
30. Matt 23:33			x	x			
31. Matt 26:10	x			x		x	
32. Matt 26:40	x	x				x	
33. Matt 26:53-54		x	x	x			x
34. Matt 26:55			x	x			
35. Matt 27:46					x	x	x
36. Mark 2:8	x	x		x		x	x
37. Mark 4:21				x		x	x
38. Mark 5:30		x				x	x
39. Mark 5:39		x		x		x	
40. Mark 7:18		x		x			
41. Mark 8:12				x			
42. Mark 8:17-18		x		x			
43. Mark 8:19		x		x			
44. Mark 8:23		x		x			x
45. Mark 9:23		x	x	x			x
46. Mark 9:50			x				
47. Mark 10:3		x	x				
48. Mark 13:2		x		x			
49. Mark 14:37			x				x
50. Luke 2:49		x	x		x		x
51. Luke 5:22-23		x		x			
52. Luke 6:46		x	x				
53. Luke 8:25			x				x
54. Luke 8:30			x				

COACHING VALUES CHART CATEGORIES (continued)	Value 1 Believe in Others	Value 2 God Initiates Change	Value 3 Individual Responsibility	Value 4 Transformation is Experiential	Value 5 Authentic Relationships	Value 6 Unique Design	Value 7 See Others Like Father Does
55. Luke 8:45	x		x	x			
56. Luke 10.15			x				x
57. Luke 10:26			x				x
58. Luke 10:36			x				x
59. Luke 11:40			x				x
60. Luke 12:14			x				
61. Luke 12:26				x			x
62. Luke 12:57			x				x
63. Luke 14:31			x		x		
64. Luke 16:11			x				
65. Luke 17:17-18			x	x			
66. Luke 18:7		x			x		
67. Luke 18:8			x		x		x
68. Luke 22:27			x				x
69. Luke 22:46			x				x
70. Luke 23:31			x				x
71. Luke 24:17			x	x	x		x
72. Luke 24:26					x		
73. Luke 24:41		x		x	x		
74. John 1:38	x			x	x		
75. John 2:4					x	x	
76. John 3:10			x	x			x
77. John 3:12		x	x				x
78. John 5:6			x				x
79. John 5:44		x	x		x		
80. John 5:47			x				x
81. John 6:5			x				x
82. John 6:61-62		x		x			
83. John 6:67			x		x		
84. John 7:19			x				x
85. John 8:10	x	x					x
86. John 8:43			x				x
87. John 8:46			x				x
88. John 8:46					x		

COACHING VALUES CHART CATEGORIES (continued)	Value 1 Believe in Others	Value 2 God Initiates Change	Value 3 Individual Responsibility	Value 4 Transformation is Experiential	Value 5 Authentic Relationships	Value 6 Unique Design	Value 7 See Others Like Father Does
89. John 11:9				x			x
90. John 11:26				x	x		x
91. John 13:12	x				x		x
92. John 14:9				x	x		x
93. John 18:4			x				x
94. John 18:11				x	x		
95. John 18:23			x				x
96. John 18:34			x				x
97. John 20:29			x	x		x	x
98. John 21:16-17	x		x		x	x	x
99. John 21:22	x		x		x	x	x
100. John 21:23	x		x		x	x	x

Biblical Theology Chart of Questions Jesus Asked

BIBLICAL THEOLOGY CHART CATEGORIES	Incarnation	Transformation	Edification	Equip	Formation	Identity	Dreams/Vision/Purpose	Honor
1. Matt 5:47	x	x				x		x
2. Matt 6:27	x	x	x	x		x		
3. Matt 6:28		x	x	x		x		
4. Matt 7:3	x	x			x			x
5. Matt 7:16	x	x				x		
6. Matt 8:26		x		x	x	x		
7. Matt 9:4	x	x			x	x		
8. Matt 9:15	x	x				x		
9. Matt 9:28	x	x	x	x				
10. Matt 11:8-9	x	x		x	x	x	x	
11. Matt 11:16		x				x	x	
12. Matt 12:11-12				x	x			
13. Matt 12:29	x	x	x	x		x		
14. Matt 12:34		x				x	x	
15. Matt 12:48		x	x		x	x		
16. Matt 14:31	x	x	x		x		x	
17. Matt 15:3		x			x	x		
18. Matt 15:34		x		x	x		x	
19. Matt 16:8	x			x	x			
20. Matt 16:13		x		x	x	x		
21. Matt 16:15	x	x	x	x	x	x	x	
22. Matt 16:26		x					x	
23. Matt 17:17					x	x	x	
24. Matt 19:17		x		x			x	x

BIBLICAL THEOLOGY CHART CATEGORIES (continued)	Incarnation	Transformation	Edification	Equip	Formation	Identity	Dreams/Vision/Purpose	Honor
25. Matt 20:22	x	x		x	x		x	
26. Matt 20:32	x	x	x				x	x
27. Matt 21:42		x					x	
28. Matt 22:18		x						
29. Matt 23:17-19		x						
30. Matt 23:33		x						
31. Matt 26:10						x		
32. Matt 26:40				x				
33. Matt 26:53-54	x					x	x	
34. Matt 26:55		x						
35. Matt 27:46						x		
36. Mark 2:8						x		
37. Mark 4:21		x						
38. Mark 5:30					x			
39. Mark 5:39						x		
40. Mark 7:18					x			
41. Mark 8:12	x						x	
42. Mark 8:17-18		x			x			
43. Mark 8:19		x			x			
44. Mark 8:23		x					x	
45. Mark 9:23					x		x	
46. Mark 9:50					x			
47. Mark 10:3		x						
48. Mark 13:2	x				x			
49. Mark 14:37				x	x		x	
50. Luke 2:49		x			x	x		
51. Luke 5:22-23	x				x			
52. Luke 6:46	x				x			
53. Luke 8:25	x	x		x			x	
54. Luke 8:30	x	x						
55. Luke 8:45	x	x						x
56. Luke 10.15						x		
57. Luke 10:26				x	x			x
58. Luke 10:36		x		x		x		
59. Luke 11:40		x					x	
60. Luke 12:14						x	x	
61. Luke 12:26				x	x			
62. Luke 12:57	x	x						
63. Luke 14:31				x	x			

BIBLICAL THEOLOGY CHART CATEGORIES (continued)	Incarnation	Transformation	Edification	Equip	Formation	Identity	Dreams/Vision/Purpose	Honor
64. Luke 16:11		x			x			
65. Luke 17:17-18	x							x
66. Luke 18:7							x	x
67. Luke 18:8					x		x	
68. Luke 22:27	x	x				x		x
69. Luke 22:46				x		x		
70. Luke 23:31						x	x	
71. Luke 24:17		x		x			x	
72. Luke 24:26	x	x		x			x	
73. Luke 24:41	x						x	x
74. John 1:38				x		x		x
75. John 2:4						x	x	x
76. John 3:10	x	x					x	x
77. John 3:12		x		x				
78. John 5:6	x						x	x
79. John 5:44	x					x		
80. John 5:47	x					x		
81. John 6:5				x		x	x	
82. John 6:61-62	x				x	x		
83. John 6:67					x	x		
84. John 7:19	x					x		
85. John 8:10			x					x
86. John 8:43	x					x		
87. John 8:46	x					x		
88. John 8:46				x	x			x
89. John 11:9								x
90. John 11:26		x			x		x	
91. John 13:12	x			x				x
92. John 14:9	x				x			
93. John 18:4						x	x	
94. John 18:11	x					x	x	x
95. John 18:23						x	x	x
96. John 18:34	x					x	x	x
97. John 20:29	x			x		x	x	
98. John 21:16-17		x	x			x		x
99. John 21:22		x				x	x	
100. John 21:23		x				x	x	

Appendix E

Example of Context & Content Explanation

Questions 26 – 32 Contributed by Tom Martin

The 100 Questions of Jesus the Master Coach reveal the different mindsets, agendas, or group cultures that he faced in these conversations. Jesus asks the questions of these "clients," and to faithfully discern what the question asks, we must determine who the primary client is to whom Jesus is asking the question. Many of these questions seek to identify how the client has assimilated what Jesus has taught, by word or deed.

The clients are identified in several categories. Here they are:

1. His disciples, that close inner, intimate group of 12 (further subdivided into the three—Peter, James and John—and the remaining eight with the one lone betrayer).
2. Those who followed closely at another level (such as those present at Pentecost)
3. Those who were primarily interested in the "show" (the miracles, healings, dealing with demonic possession, signs, and wonders)
4. Those who were opponents bent on defeating Jesus at every turn (mostly among the religious leaders who had to stand with the Roman government and who did not want to see any significant changes to their lot).
5. Those of us who are reading the passages of the gospels. Likewise, this group can be divided into groupings: inquirer(s), follower(s)/believer(s), and antagonist(s).

Each question that Jesus presents is considered by which client group He is directly addressing in the life events of the moment as recorded, as well as its impact on those of us who are reading the account, and how our faith development impacts our reactions. Here is a list of 12 of these questions that break this down as a model of how to approach any of the 100 Jesus questions in the gospels. The numbering of these questions corresponds to the list given in the 100 Questions list.

Also, each question is assigned a coaching core value(s) described in detail in Chapter 1. Finally, each question is assigned a biblical core value or theological principle that is described in Chapters 5 and 6 and is color-coded on the website that is part of this publication.

Coaching Core Values (from Chapter 1)

"Believing in Others"

"Find where God is initiating Change."

"Reinforce their own-life stewardship."

"Recognize transformation is primarily experiential."

"Catalyze Authenticity to build Trust."

"Celebrate other's Uniqueness."

"See others as our Father sees."

Biblical Core Values (from Chapters 5 & 6)

Incarnation   Phil. 2:6-8

Transformation   Rom. 12:2

Edification   Rom. 14:19

Equip   Eph. 4:11-12

Identity/Formation   Ps. 139:13-15; Gal.3:28; Jn. 10:3-5

Dreams/Vision   Jn. 12:27

Honor   Deut. 5:16

Based on this model of 12 questions entirely given in their context, readers can then look at the charts that categorize all of the 100 questions with a greater depth of appreciation.

26. What do you want me to do for you? (Matthew 20:32)

Full Verse: Matthew 20:32

[32] So Jesus stood still and called them, and said, "What do you want Me to do for you?"

Full Context of the incident: Matthew 20:29-34

[29] Now as they went out of Jericho, a great multitude followed Him.

³⁰ And behold, two blind men sitting by the road, when they heard that Jesus was passing by, cried out, saying, "Have mercy on us, O Lord, Son of David!"

³¹ Then the multitude warned them that they should be quiet; but they cried out all the more, saying, "Have mercy on us, O Lord, Son of David!"

³² So Jesus stood still and called them, and said, "What do you want Me to do for you?"

³³ They said to Him, "Lord, that our eyes may be opened."

³⁴ So Jesus had compassion and touched their eyes. And immediately their eyes received sight, and they followed Him.

Client(s): Two blind men; the multitude following Jesus, the disciples with Him. Finally, those of us who are reading the interchange.

Core Coaching Value(s)

Believing in People/God Initiates Change/Each Person Is Unique/ Transformation Happens Experientially:

Jesus believed in the two men and initiated a radical change in their lives. He demonstrated compassion and, having the supernatural ability to effect change, He acts to relieve their personal, unique dilemma. This event records a real-life change in the two men. Healing of a blind person involves much more than simply receiving sight. There is a complete reprogramming of the 'seeing' portion of the brain which includes the upload of a complete database of visual images that before this encounter with Jesus did not exist in each man's brain. Therefore, each man received a complete library of visual images so that when the eyes as sensors recorded an image, their brains had a thorough reference library to which the images could be matched. Thus, the healing miracle was complete, and they could see.

Ministry Flows Out of Incarnational Being: The act of healing was a frequent action Jesus took that identified Who He was and provided authentication to those who followed Him as well as those of us reading the account.

Authentic Relationship: How many times do we experience Almighty God directly asking us 'what He can do for us?' Jesus, our coach, seeks to effect change in our lives through our relationship with Him. The two men after receiving their sight followed Jesus. The outcome of this 'coach' interaction was the demonstration of the faith of the two men as they believed in what Jesus could do, experienced a dramatic change, and then proceeded to follow Him.

27. Did you never read the scriptures? (Matthew 21:42)

Full Verse: Matthew 21:42

42 Jesus said to them, "Have you never read in the Scriptures: 'The stone which the builders rejected Has become the chief cornerstone. This was the LORD'S doing, And it is marvelous in our eyes'?

Full Context of the incident: Matthew 21:33-46

33 "Hear another parable: There was a certain landowner who planted a vineyard and set a hedge around it, dug a winepress in it and built a tower. And he leased it to vinedressers and went into a far country.

34 Now when vintage-time drew near, he sent his servants to the vinedressers, that they might receive its fruit.

35 And the vinedressers took his servants, beat one, killed one, and stoned another.

36 Again he sent other servants, more than the first, and they did likewise to them.

37 Then last of all he sent his son to them, saying, 'They will respect my son.'

38 But when the vinedressers saw the son, they said among themselves, 'This is the heir. Come, let us kill him and seize his inheritance.'

39 So they took him and cast him out of the vineyard and killed him.

40 Therefore, when the owner of the vineyard comes, what will he do to those vinedressers?"

41 They said to Him, "He will destroy those wicked men miserably, and lease his vineyard to other vinedressers who will render to him the fruits in their seasons."

42 Jesus said to them, "Have you never read in the Scriptures: 'The stone which the builders rejected Has become the chief

cornerstone. This was the LORD'S doing, And it is marvelous in our eyes'?"

⁴³ "Therefore I say to you, the kingdom of God will be taken from you and given to a nation bearing the fruits of it.

⁴⁴ And whoever falls on this stone will be broken; but on whomever it falls, it will grind him to powder."

⁴⁵ Now when the chief priests and Pharisees heard His parables, they perceived that He was speaking of them.

⁴⁶ But when they sought to lay hands on Him, they feared the multitudes, because they took Him for a prophet.

Client(s): Chief Priests and Pharisees, disciples who heard and recorded the discourse, and, finally, we as readers.

Core Coaching Value(s)

God Initiates Change/Leaders Take Responsibility: Jesus initiates change in the midst of an ongoing conversation between Him and the religious leaders of Israel. He takes episodes from real life in the form of parables to state principles of God's kingdom to the so-called leaders of the religious/spiritual life of the nation. The discourse takes place on the Temple courts in the week preceding His arrest, trial, and conviction. His question comes in response to rather emphatic truth-telling statements by the religious leaders who have spoken rightly about the story Jesus is telling, not realizing that they are proclaiming their demise. The coach seeks to have the client realize the true reality of the circumstances of life.

Jesus' telling of the parable and using their reaction to pronounce the consequences of their leadership diverted them from their first purpose which was to take Him prisoner. They could not move against Him in the presence of the people.

28. Why are you testing me? (Matthew 22:18)

Full Verse: Matthew 22:18

¹⁸ But Jesus perceived their wickedness, and said, "Why do you test Me, you hypocrites?

Full Context of the incident: Matthew 22:15-22

¹⁵ Then the Pharisees went and plotted how they might entangle Him in His talk.
¹⁶ And they sent to Him their disciples with the Herodians, saying, "Teacher, we know that You are true, and teach the way of God in truth; nor do You care about anyone, for You do not regard the person of men.
¹⁷ Tell us, therefore, what do You think? Is it lawful to pay taxes to Caesar, or not?"
¹⁸ But Jesus perceived their wickedness, and said, "Why do you test Me, you hypocrites?
¹⁹ Show Me the tax money." So, they brought Him a denarius.
²⁰ And He said to them, "Whose image and inscription is this?"
²¹ They said to Him, "Caesar's." And He said to them, "Render therefore to Caesar the things that are Caesar's, and to God the things that are God's."
²² When they had heard these words, they marveled, and left Him and went their way.

Client(s): Religious leaders, disciples, and the readers.

Core Coaching Value(s)

God Initiates Change/Leaders Take Responsibility/Transformation Happens Experientially: Jesus confronts the worldview of the clients and addresses their practices. They profess a belief in God and adhere to a concept of truth, but their goal is to discredit what they see Jesus do and say. What they profess to believe is not what they do. Thus, He addresses them as 'hypocrites'. As it is said, 'What we do is what we believe; everything else is religious talk.'

Believing in People: Jesus responds to people directly, going to the truth that is in their person: body, soul, and spirit. To do otherwise would demonstrate a lack of sincere interest in the person. The coach seeks to understand what God is looking to change in the client and addresses that issue directly, focusing on the 'why' of the client's current situation and what the client perceives as a potential direction toward change.

Transformation is Experiential: The 'clients' were attacking the very identity of who Jesus was. The gospel writers expressed Jesus' perception of the 'wickedness' in the motivation of His accusers. Jesus asks the religious leaders to justify the reason for their questioning, identifying them as hypocrites. The coach seeks to assist the client to recognize his true identity which will result in action to achieve the desired change.

God Initiates Change: Jesus takes charge of the situation, identifying the false, wicked motives of His accusers and working them through a real-life experience that illustrates the case they present is false. They create a question to attempt to trap Jesus such that He cannot answer them. The significant result in this encounter is that Jesus reveals to them that their assumptions are false: they present the problem as an 'either/or' life situation, when, in fact, Jesus demonstrates that it is 'both/and' reality of life. We honor both God and the government He ordained.

29. Blind fools, which is greater, the gold or the temple that makes the goal sacred...the gift or the altar that makes the gift sacred? (Matthew 23:17-19)

Full Verse: Matthew 23:17-19

¹⁷ Fools and blind! For which is greater, the gold or the temple that sanctifies the gold?

¹⁸ And, 'Whoever swears by the altar, it is nothing; but whoever swears by the gift that is on it, he is obliged to perform it.'

¹⁹ Fools and blind!

Full context of the incident: Matthew 23:1-36

¹ Then Jesus spoke to the multitudes and to His disciples,

² saying: "The scribes and the Pharisees sit in Moses' seat.

³ Therefore whatever they tell you to observe, that observe and do, but do not do according to their works; for they say, and do not do.

⁴ For they bind heavy burdens, hard to bear, and lay them on men's shoulders; but they themselves will not move them with one of their fingers.

⁵ But all their works they do to be seen by men. They make their phylacteries broad and enlarge the borders of their garments.

⁶ They love the best places at feasts, the best seats in the synagogues,

⁷ greetings in the marketplaces, and to be called by men, 'Rabbi, Rabbi.'

⁸ But you, do not be called 'Rabbi'; for One is your Teacher, the Christ, and you are all brethren.

⁹ Do not call anyone on earth your father; for One is your Father, He who is in heaven.

¹⁰ And do not be called teachers; for One is your Teacher, the Christ.

¹¹ But he who is greatest among you shall be your servant.

¹² And whoever exalts himself will be humbled, and he who humbles himself will be exalted.

¹³ But woe to you, scribes and Pharisees, hypocrites! For you shut up the kingdom of heaven against men; for you neither go in yourselves, nor do you allow those who are entering to go in.

¹⁴ Woe to you, scribes and Pharisees, hypocrites! For you devour widows' houses, and for a pretense make long prayers. Therefore, you will receive greater condemnation.

¹⁵ Woe to you, scribes and Pharisees, hypocrites! For you travel land and sea to win one proselyte, and when he is won, you make him twice as much a son of hell as yourselves.

¹⁶ Woe to you, blind guides, who say, 'Whoever swears by the temple, it is nothing; but whoever swears by the gold of the temple, he is obliged to perform it.'

¹⁷ Fools and blind! For which is greater, the gold or the temple that sanctifies the gold?

¹⁸ And, 'Whoever swears by the altar, it is nothing; but whoever swears by the gift that is on it, he is obliged to perform it.'

¹⁹ Fools and blind! For which is greater, the gift or the altar that sanctifies the gift?

²⁰ Therefore he who swears by the altar, swears by it and by all things on it.

²¹ He who swears by the temple, swears by it and by Him who dwells in it.

²² And he who swears by heaven, swears by the throne of God and by Him who sits on it.

²³ Woe to you, scribes and Pharisees, hypocrites! For you pay tithe of mint and anise and cummin and have neglected the weightier matters of the law: justice and mercy and faith. These you ought to have done, without leaving the others undone.

²⁴ Blind guides, who strain out a gnat and swallow a camel!

²⁵ Woe to you, scribes and Pharisees, hypocrites! For you cleanse the outside of the cup and dish, but inside they are full of extortion and self-indulgence.

²⁶ Blind Pharisee first cleanse the inside of the cup and dish, that the outside of them may be clean also.

²⁷ Woe to you, scribes and Pharisees, hypocrites! For you are like whitewashed tombs which indeed appear beautiful outwardly, but inside are full of dead men's bones and all uncleanness.

²⁸ Even so you also outwardly appear righteous to men, but inside you are full of hypocrisy and lawlessness.

²⁹ Woe to you, scribes and Pharisees, hypocrites! Because you build the tombs of the prophets and adorn the monuments of the righteous,

³⁰ and say, 'If we had lived in the days of our fathers, we would not have been partakers with them in the blood of the prophets.'

³¹ Therefore you are witnesses against yourselves that you are sons of those who murdered the prophets.

³² Fill up, then, the measure of your father's' guilt.

³³ Serpents, brood of vipers! How can you escape the condemnation of hell?

³⁴ Therefore, indeed, I send you prophets, wise men, and scribes: some of them you will kill and crucify, and some of them you will scourge in your synagogues and persecute from city to city,

³⁵ that on you may come all the righteous blood shed on the earth, from the blood of righteous Abel to the blood of Zechariah, son of Berechiah, whom you murdered between the temple and the altar.

³⁶ Assuredly, I say to you, all these things will come upon this generation.

Client(s): Disciples and readers regarding the scribes and Pharisees

Core Coaching Value(s)

Transformation is Experiential: Jesus declares the very identity of the 'clients.' "Fools" is the grammatical noun of the statement and identifies the basic nature or character of His accusers. Many would be considered to be a 'fool,' and Jesus adds an adjective, "blind," to describe a particular crippling condition to their fundamental nature. They have all the trappings of a religious community that worships the activity and not the objective of their beliefs. Their activity reveals a lack of true faith. They are more interested in conforming to practice that is superficial; not a worship of spirit and truth. Jesus calls them to specifically and carefully chose between true and false worship.

Seeing others as the Father does: Jesus recites the daily life actions of the 'clients' which exposes the false living of the religious leaders. While Jesus is addressing His disciples and the multitudes who were following Him, He points out the practices of the religious leaders and how they focus on the tools of worship and not the spiritual heart of true worship. The 'blindness' equate to the state of spiritual blindness which prohibits our clearly understanding the real revelation from God. We are being warned by looking at the life of the religious leaders as a clear example of what not to do. Therefore, the coach is careful to guide the client in truth-seeking so that the goals desired are compatible with the truth and fulfill a purpose-driven life.

30. How are you to avoid being sentenced to hell? (Matthew 23:33)

Full Verse: Matthew 23:33

³³ Serpents, brood of vipers! How can you escape the condemnation of hell?

Full context of the incident: Matthew 23:1-36

¹ Then Jesus spoke to the multitudes and to His disciples,

² saying: "The scribes and the Pharisees sit in Moses' seat.

[3] Therefore whatever they tell you to observe, that observe and do, but do not do according to their works; for they say, and do not do.

[4] For they bind heavy burdens, hard to bear, and lay them on men's shoulders; but they themselves will not move them with one of their fingers.

[5] But all their works they do to be seen by men. They make their phylacteries broad and enlarge the borders of their garments.

[6] They love the best places at feasts, the best seats in the synagogues,

[7] greetings in the marketplaces, and to be called by men, 'Rabbi, Rabbi.'

[8] But you, do not be called 'Rabbi'; for One is your Teacher, the Christ, and you are all brethren.

[9] Do not call anyone on earth your father; for One is your Father, He who is in heaven.

[10] And do not be called teachers; for One is your Teacher, the Christ.

[11] But he who is greatest among you shall be your servant.

[12] And whoever exalts himself will be humbled, and he who humbles himself will be exalted.

[13] But woe to you, scribes and Pharisees, hypocrites! For you shut up the kingdom of heaven against men; for you neither go in yourselves, nor do you allow those who are entering to go in.

[14] Woe to you, scribes and Pharisees, hypocrites! For you devour widows' houses, and for a pretense make long prayers. Therefore, you will receive greater condemnation.

[15] Woe to you, scribes and Pharisees, hypocrites! For you travel land and sea to win one proselyte, and when he is won, you make him twice as much a son of hell as yourselves.

[16] Woe to you, blind guides, who say, 'Whoever swears by the temple, it is nothing; but whoever swears by the gold of the temple, he is obliged to perform it.'

[17] Fools and blind! For which is greater, the gold or the temple that sanctifies the gold?

¹⁸ And, 'Whoever swears by the altar, it is nothing; but whoever swears by the gift that is on it, he is obliged to perform it.'

¹⁹ Fools and blind! For which is greater, the gift or the altar that sanctifies the gift?

²⁰ Therefore he who swears by the altar, swears by it and by all things on it.

²¹ He who swears by the temple, swears by it and by Him who dwells in it.

²² And he who swears by heaven, swears by the throne of God and by Him who sits on it.

²³ Woe to you, scribes and Pharisees, hypocrites! For you pay tithe of mint and anise and cummin and have neglected the weightier matters of the law: justice and mercy and faith. These you ought to have done, without leaving the others undone.

²⁴ Blind guides, who strain out a gnat and swallow a camel!

²⁵ Woe to you, scribes and Pharisees, hypocrites! For you cleanse the outside of the cup and dish, but inside they are full of extortion and self-indulgence.

²⁶ Blind Pharisee first cleanse the inside of the cup and dish, that the outside of them may be clean also.

²⁷ Woe to you, scribes and Pharisees, hypocrites! For you are like whitewashed tombs which indeed appear beautiful outwardly, but inside are full of dead men's bones and all uncleanness.

²⁸ Even so you also outwardly appear righteous to men, but inside you are full of hypocrisy and lawlessness.

²⁹ Woe to you, scribes and Pharisees, hypocrites! Because you build the tombs of the prophets and adorn the monuments of the righteous,

³⁰ and say, 'If we had lived in the days of our fathers, we would not have been partakers with them in the blood of the prophets.'

³¹ Therefore you are witnesses against yourselves that you are sons of those who murdered the prophets.

³² Fill up, then, the measure of your father's' guilt.

³³ Serpents, brood of vipers! How can you escape the condemnation of hell?

³⁴ Therefore, indeed, I send you prophets, wise men, and scribes: some of them you will kill and crucify, and some of them you will scourge in your synagogues and persecute from city to city,

³⁵ that on you may come all the righteous blood shed on the earth, from the blood of righteous Abel to the blood of Zechariah, son of Berechiah, whom you murdered between the temple and the altar.

³⁶ Assuredly, I say to you, all these things will come upon this generation.

Client(s): Disciples, followers, and readers with reference to the practices of the religious leaders.

Core Coaching Value(s)

Leaders take responsibility for their own lives: Jesus warns His followers and disciples that the life they see being lived out by the religious rulers is false. The scribes and Pharisees live their lives precisely opposite to what God has instructed in His Word and Law. He begins this discourse by instructing what is correct and at the same time pointing out that the leaders say what Moses taught all the while not carrying out his instruction. Jesus gives a classic principle: do what they say, not what they do. Then He begins a series of "Woes" that dispel any notion that what the scribes and Pharisees do is of any eternal value. And the result of these prescriptions leads to the question of "How can [they] avoid the condemnation of hell?"

Transformation Happens Experientially: Jesus stresses to His followers and disciples that there is a correct way to live our lives and that is to become a servant. There will be many who like the scribes and Pharisees will come to the judgment thinking that they have been doing a great work only to find out that they were working to their advantage for this life with no concern for eternity. The coach guides the client through experiences that will develop the servant's heart and avoid the useless collection of wasted experiences.

31. Why do you make trouble for the woman? (Matthew 26:10)

Full Verse: Matthew 26:10

> [10] But when Jesus was aware of it, He said to them, "Why do you trouble the woman? For she has done a good work for Me.

Full context of the incident: Matthew 26:1-13

> [1] Now it came to pass, when Jesus had finished all these sayings, that He said to His disciples,
>
> [2] "You know that after two days is the Passover, and the Son of Man will be delivered up to be crucified."
>
> [3] Then the chief priests, the scribes, and the elders of the people assembled at the palace of the high priest, who was called Caiaphas,
>
> [4] and plotted to take Jesus by trickery and kill Him.
>
> [5] But they said, "Not during the feast, lest there be an uproar among the people."
>
> [6] And when Jesus was in Bethany at the house of Simon the leper,
>
> [7] a woman came to Him having an alabaster flask of very costly fragrant oil, and she poured it on His head as He sat at the table.
>
> [8] But when His disciples saw it, they were indignant, saying, "Why this waste?
>
> [9] For this fragrant oil might have been sold for much and given to the poor."
>
> [10] But when Jesus was aware of it, He said to them, "Why do you trouble the woman? For she has done a good work for Me.
>
> [11] For you have the poor with you always, but Me you do not have always.
>
> [12] For in pouring this fragrant oil on My body, she did it for My burial.
>
> [13] Assuredly, I say to you, wherever this gospel is preached in the whole world, what this woman has done will also be told as a memorial to her."

Client(s): Disciples, followers and the readers

Core Coaching Value(s)

Believing in People/Transformation Happens Experientially/Leaders Take Responsibility/Each Person Is Unique:

104

Jesus hears the grumbling of His disciples and others that were with them concerning the actions of a woman. Even having listened to the teachings of Jesus and His words to the religious leaders, the disciples chose to question the acts of worship of this woman. Their actions focused on material work rather than a work of worship. Yes, in this world, there will always be a need to help others, and each of us should do so. Jesus saw the heart and spirit of this woman, and as He said, we have all read about her selfless act of worship just before His arrest. As a coach we need to be aware of the motives of our clients, trusting that the Holy Spirit will reveal to us what is/are the motive(s) of the person's heart. It is far too easy to misjudge and react too quickly to another's actions.

32. Could you not watch with me one brief hour? (Matthew 26:40)

Full Verse: Matthew 26:40

⁴⁰ Then He came to the disciples and found them asleep, and said to Peter, "What? Could you not watch with Me one hour?

Full context of the incident: Matthew 26:31-46

³¹ Then Jesus said to them, "All of you will be made to stumble because of Me this night, for it is written: 'I will strike the Shepherd, And the sheep of the flock will be scattered.'

³² But after I have been raised, I will go before you to Galilee."

³³ Peter answered and said to Him, "Even if all are made to stumble because of You, I will never be made to stumble."

³⁴ Jesus said to him, "Assuredly, I say to you that this night, before the rooster crows, you will deny Me three times."

³⁵ Peter said to Him, "Even if I have to die with You, I will not deny You!" And so said all the disciples.

³⁶ Then Jesus came with them to a place called Gethsemane, and said to the disciples, "Sit here while I go and pray over there."

³⁷ And He took with Him Peter and the two sons of Zebedee, and He began to be sorrowful and deeply distressed.

³⁸ Then He said to them, "My soul is exceedingly sorrowful, even to death. Stay here and watch with Me."

³⁹ He went a little farther and fell on His face, and prayed, saying, "O My Father, if it is possible, let this cup pass from Me; nevertheless, not as I will, but as You will."

⁴⁰ Then He came to the disciples and found them asleep, and said to Peter, "What? Could you not watch with Me one hour?

⁴¹ Watch and pray, lest you enter into temptation. The spirit indeed is willing, but the flesh is weak."

⁴² Again, a second time, He went away and prayed, saying, "O My Father, if this cup cannot pass away from Me unless I drink it, Your will be done."

⁴³ And He came and found them asleep again, for their eyes were heavy.

⁴⁴ So He left them, went away again, and prayed the third time, saying the same words.

⁴⁵ Then He came to His disciples and said to them, "Are you still sleeping and resting? Behold, the hour is at hand, and the Son of Man is being betrayed into the hands of sinners.

⁴⁶ Rise, let us be going. See, My betrayer is at hand."

Client(s): Disciples and readers.

Core Coaching Value(s)

Believing in People/God Initiates Change/Each Person Is Unique

Jesus awakens Peter and asks him to remain awake, just for a short time. While He sees that all the disciples are sleeping, it is Peter to whom He speaks and admonishes. He knows Peter; He has a great purpose for him; He realizes that Peter along with every one of us have physical weaknesses that no matter how much we may desire to be strong for ministry and worship, our energy level and motivation will not sustain us. It seems that by His actions, Jesus is asking Peter (and us) to be with Him and at the same time demonstrating an understanding that we will not be able to do so. We know that in the future the time will be redeemed as we 'watch and pray.' The coach gauges the physical abilities of the client and measures how he can guide the client to a position of strength and perseverance.

Free Resources &
Training Opportunities

FREE RESOURCES FOR
BREAKTHROUGH CONVERSATIONS

DOWNLOAD THESE FREE BOOKS
AND SIGN UP FOR MORE INFORMATION HERE

https://lifeforming.net/2freebooks

Conversational Champions

Credentialing Trainers to enable anyone to have life-changing interactions anywhere, anytime

"Are you a church leader/facilitator that wants to train your members to change the quality of family and workplace conversations? Do you want to empower your members to transform the small talk and polarized talk they face every day to real, authentic, and honoring conversations?

Conversational Champions Certification
will qualify you to have the competence and confidence so you can:

- Help parents connect relationally with their kids
- Help spouses communicate authentically with one another
- Empower church members to rekindle purpose and passion in their interactions
- Equip leaders to make conflict less damaging and more productive
- Train workers to turn boring meetings into highly engaging experiences
- Create immediate transformation stories of impact in the community

8-WEEK LIVE & ONLINE COURSE

Four weeks into your 8-week course you will be excited to launch your first "Conversational Champion" group and begin hearing the stories of breakthrough at home and work. You or your church can equip your people, have an ongoing income stream, and weekly testimonies from excited members in their homes and workplaces.

Your mission, if you choose to accept it, is to become a certified facilitator that changes the conversation and relationship quality within your church and community in 8 weeks or less and receive an income stream from your ongoing training. Check out a sample video clip:

https://drive.google.com/open?id=175K8fPXkos3P6aSGtOE2t_M51JwBICFq

REGISTER HERE

http://www.lifeforminginstitute.com/course/conversational-champions/

108

"Master Communicator Certification" is a live online 12 Week Communication Training Program that provides 3 Certifications in one.

1. ## Conversation Champion Certification:
   Credentialing Trainers to enable anyone to have life-changing interactions anywhere anytime

2. ## Workplace Coach Certification: Credentialing
   Staff & Leaders in the best of practical coaching conversations for the workplace

3. ## Master Coach APP Certification: Acquire the
   Master Coach 3D Coaching Methodology to help others play to their strengths, take positive action and win results

"We certify leaders, managers, supervisors, board members, staff, in business, non-profits and churches, to train their members for breakthrough conversations at home and at work."

REGISTER HERE

http://lifeforminginstitute.com/mastercommunicator

Accelerated Coach Training

A Systematic, Effective Method to Develop Coaches and Leaders with Character and Competence for professional leadership coaching.

- Define the Professional Coaching Paradigm
- Develop the Heart & Values of a Transformational Coach
- Learn to Listen Discerningly and Ask More Powerful Questions
- Develop Healthy Authentic Relationships & a Culture of Honor
- Learn Proven Models for Coaching Conversations
- Gain a Coaching Approach to Change and Growth in people and organizations
- Setup and Build a Coaching Relationship with Feedback and Supervision

The ACT Program is an in-depth, 15-week program designed for those who desire to use competencies either as a professional coach or professionally in their current role. It employs a combination of two two-day workshops, eight group sessions, eight personal coaching sessions with a peer coach and/or coach trainer, as well as working with a client, for a thoroughly experiential coach training process which also creates personal transformation in the lives of the trainees.

ACT training uses a live virtual format. You will work with a Trainer, a cohort peer, online resources and personal study with exercises. Trainees do not need to travel, you only need to have access to a computer and long-distance calling.

REGISTER HERE

https://www.lifeforminginstitute.com/course/accelerated-coach-training/

AMBASSADOR
— A S S O C I A T I O N —

Credentialing, Positioning, & Leveraging a global movement of High-Impact Influencers

www.ambassadorassociation.com

Dr. Joseph Umidi has always been intrigued by the role of Ambassadors to a nation; how they are trained, how the best of them are able to create milestone memories at key moments in difficult conversations. When he discovered over 550 people whose lives were altered by one personal conversation with an Ambassador over his four-year tenure in the U.S., he knew he had found his life calling. In 1999 he started Lifeforming, a training organization to train leaders with Ambassador quality skills that has become an international movement of over 10,000 certified relational leaders in 31 countries and 14 languages. His 32 years of teaching at Master and Doctoral levels at Regent University, including roles as Dean and now as Executive Vice President, have given him opportunities to interact with present and emerging global Ambassadors. In 2017 he launched the Ambassador Association, a membership platform for helping hundreds of influential leaders maximize their Personal Leadership Effectiveness through unique coaching clusters and cutting-edge technology.

MORE INFORMATION ON MEMBERSHIP OR SPEAKER REQUEST:

https://www.goresearch.me/ambassadorassociation

https://www.goresearch.me/josephumidi

MasterCoach App
Growing People & Performance

1. Our APP

- World's First Action-based Coaching App
- 3 Powerful Steps to Help Others Succeed:
  - DISCOVER & Activate Strengths
  - DEVELOP Insights-led Actions
  - DEDICATE to Follow Through

2. Our PROGRAMME

- Develop Leaders as 'Ambassador Communicators'
- Online or Onsite Workshop
- Gain Proven Workplace Coaching Skills
- Learn to Coach with the MasterCoach App

Use our 'App + Training' Solution to Build a **High Performance Culture** in your Business

info@ambassadorassociation.com

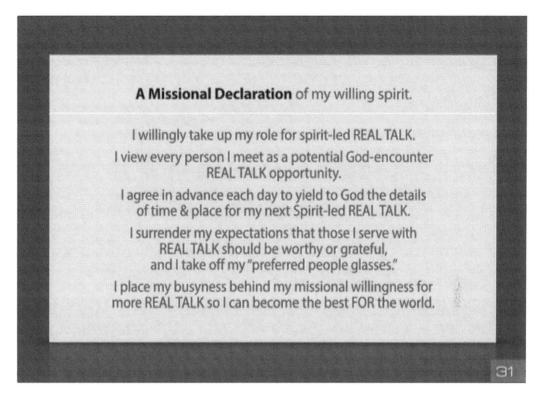

If you are willing to make this declaration every-day for 1 week YOU will see a new level of conversational breakthrough in your life. WE want to hear your stories of what happens and publish the Jesus Master Coach approach to the nations. Submit yours to:

info@lifeforminginstitute.com